Happy bi[illegible]

Much lo[illegible]

A Joy Forever

A Treasury of Quotations with Comments
from the favourite writers of

PATIENCE STRONG

MOWBRAYS
LONDON & OXFORD

Printed in Great Britain by
Alden & Mowbray Ltd
at the Alden Press, Oxford

ISBN 0 264 64607 X

First published 1973
by A. R. Mowbray & Co Ltd
The Alden Press, Osney Mead
Oxford OX2 0EF

ACKNOWLEDGEMENTS

I acknowledge with thanks, permission to quote from the following: *Precious Bane* by Mary Webb; *Le Milieu Divin* by Pierre Teilhard de Chardin; *The Story of Thomas More* by John Farrow; *Journals of Dorothy Wordsworth*, volume 1, edited by E. de Selincourt; *The Science of Thought Review* edited by Clare Cameron; and *John Wesley—Anglican* by Garth Lean.

For their kind permission to quote Harold Monro's 'Overheard On a Saltmarsh' from *An Anthology Of Recent Poetry* first published in 1920 I am indebted to Messrs George G. Harrap & Co. Ltd, and I trust that the unknown author of 'A Fisherman's Prayer' will forgive the liberty I have taken in including his poem in my collection of prayers.

If aught I've used without consent
I here make due acknowledgement.
For the trespass of omission
Be assured of my contrition
And with eye of charity
Overlook and pardon me.

CONTENTS

CHAPTER ONE

A Joy Forever

What is treasure? For some it is a cherished object that can be kept under lock and key, a ring, a brooch, a necklace or the figure on a piece of paper which represents gold in the vaults of a bank. For others treasure is something that cannot be valued in terms of money for it has to do with the riches of the mind and the affluence of the spirit. This is not to say that the acquisition of material treasures is a bad thing. The passion for beautiful furnishings and fabrics can be aesthetically satisfying. A lovely piece of embroidery, a picture, a jewel or work of art can be a precious thing in itself, regardless of its monetary value. Whatever feeds the mind with good things nourishes the soul and enriches life on every level.

True treasure is that which is prized for its own sake and not for its market value. This surely is what Keats must have had in mind when in a letter to Fanny Brawne he wrote: 'I have loved the principle of beauty in all things', a thought enshrined in the opening immortal lines of Endymion.

A thing of beauty is a joy forever:
Its loveliness increases; it will never
Pass into nothingness, but still will keep
A bower quiet for us, and a sleep
Full of sweet dreams, and health and quiet breathing.

Whatever your treasure may be, a house, a gem, a dream, a person or a thing, the Man on the Mountain spoke truly when He said, 'Where your treasure is there will your heart be also.'

My treasure is in this room where I write. Here are my bookshelves packed from floor to ceiling with the harvest of the years. Some have been sought for, some given. Many have come from I know not where to meet a need, but they each have their place on my shelves and in my life and their own peculiar blessing to bestow. None could be spared; I gloat over them as a miser counts his coins. They belong as members of a family. Books are like friends. They are drawn to us and we to them, becoming in time a part of the living texture of our intellectual and spiritual existence.

The strange manner in which certain books come to you at the moment when you are ready for what they have to give seems at times like a psychical phenomenon. The joy of discovering a new book-friend smacks of the miraculous, a joy so personal that an instantaneous relationship is established between author and reader. It is like falling in love at first sight. At last you have met. The gap is closed.

The word 'study' is too ivory-towerish to convey the right impression of this room, so I call it my workshop. It was once a garage but with the practical help of a village craftsman, a type now, alas, never to be found amongst the younger generation, I have given it a domed ceiling made in a single day with ordinary hardboard. The mass-produced plain door has been transformed by a panel of French paper in a pale shade of grey and by a china handle and finger plates with a hand-painted design of old-fashioned moss roses.

A plain cinnamon-coloured carpet picks up the pale gold stripes in the Victorian wallpaper. A signed proof print portrait of Shelley hangs over a rather lovely oil lamp which stands on an old walnut chest. When lit the lamp's soft glow lights up the precious picture which, needless to say, hangs alone on its own section of wall, and it is here that year in and year out I write or type my books, verses and letters surrounded by a diverse company of silent friends, my books. The nine white-painted groove-edged shelves, eight feet in width, stand between two windows. One, a square of twenty-eight panes with lambs'-tongue glazing bars, faces south east to the sunrising with a window box outside conventionally gay with wallflowers in Spring and geraniums in Summer. From this window I can see the ever-busy road through the trailing boughs of a willow tree. The other window, bow-shaped in a bay, looks out upon a seventy-acre cornfield with a cluster of Kentish oasthouses making a focal point across the valley with what I call their clown caps and what the old countrymen call their tongue-eye cowls, white against a dark blur of orchards and copses.

The space between these two windows holds my heart for it holds my treasure. Books of reference are kept in unobtrusive corners as far removed from the treasury as can be contrived, for this, apart from the fact that it contains my dearest possessions, is no ordinary set of bookshelves. It has its own special magic. For many years it stood in Lamb House, Rye, the home of Henry James; made no doubt by the local carpenter. I bought it with a few other things, a Georgian cupboard, a pen tray, a Majolica jar and some linen table-napkins embroidered with the initials H.J.

at an auction sale held at the time when Lamb House was about to pass into the care of the National Trust and I was living in Winchelsea.

When Henry James died in 1916 the old house with its walled garden in the corner by the church was let furnished to various tenants and finally to the distinguished Benson brothers, sons of an Archbishop of Canterbury, so the literary traditions of the house were carried on and I love to reflect upon some of the giants who, for over half a century, must have browsed among the shelves that now stand in my workshop. It is smaller than the original, as my various moves made it necessary to reduce its size. Once when I moved into an Elizabethan cottage in Sussex with small doors and low lintels the almost sacred bookcase had to stand against a wall in the garden covered in sheets until a carpenter could be found to reduce its height by eighteen inches. Many a great writer of the period must have passed through the gracious door of Lamb House and many a pilgrim in this ungracious age still climbs the steep cobbled street past the old wistaria-covered Mermaid Inn in search of the ghosts which, I like to believe, hover at times around my beloved books.

Writing on his return from Italy in 1899 to Mr Warren, the architect in charge of repairs, following what might have been a disastrous fire at Lamb House, Henry James wrote, 'Everything is perfect—the new bookcase in the drawing room perhaps the most perfect of all.' Was this, in fact, what is now my treasury? Mine could not have been the one in the Garden Room where he worked as that was completely destroyed by a German bomb in August 1940.

Sometimes at night when a full moon keeps me awake I go into the workshop and sit before my books. The silence of the silvered room is charged with a feeling of secret companionship sweeter and more intimate than conversation with a flesh-and-blood person could ever be. Books may be mute but they are alive in their power to evoke the past and interpret the present.

A collection of books is autobiographical, a silent disclosure of the secrets of its owner's reading life from phase to phase. A section of one of my shelves is devoted to books that at a touch or a glance can take me back to childhood days: a well-thumbed *Alice in Wonderland*, a *Gulliver's Travels*, Kingsley's *Water Babies*, a battered and much used *Pilgrim's Progress*, a *Foxe's Book of Martyrs*, *What Katy Did* and *What Katy Did Next*, and dearest of all a backless Tennyson, inscribed 'To my sister on her tenth birthday'. Nothing would induce me to have that poor little book rebound. Its tattered shabbiness is a mute testimony to the tenacity with which I have clung to it 'through all the changing scenes of life, in trouble and in joy'.

On the third shelf of the treasury stand the books which are reminders of my teen-age gropings after some facet of truth. *In Tune With the Infinite*, by Ralph Waldo Trine; *Science and Health With Key to the Scriptures*, by Mary Baker Eddy, Emerson's Essays, *The Gift of the Spirit*, by Prentice Mulford, *The Survival of Man*, by Sir Oliver Lodge, Thomas Troward's *Edinburgh Lectures on Mental Science*, *Natural Law in the Spiritual World*, by Henry Drummond and *Heaven and Hell*, by Swedenborg.

On the next shelf are books collected during a

movement towards an exploration into orthodox theology inspired by a growing interest in the study of British Israel teachings. William Law, Jeremy Taylor, John Donne, Simone Weil, Evelyn Underhill, Father Andrew, C. S. Lewis, Pierre Teilhard de Chardin, Thomas Merton, John Wesley, Thomas à Kempis.

On a higher shelf come the mystics, placed intentionally above the theologians and the New Thinkers as an instinctive act of reverence. Names such as Jacob Boehme, St Teresa of The Interior Castle, Richard Rolle, Julian of Norwich, St John of the Cross, Thomas Kelly, Quaker, Brother Lawrence, Baron von Hügel, *The Cloud of Unknowing* seem to cast a softening glow over the dogmas of institutional religion like light from an altar candle.

The poets occupy the two main shelves with great names flashing a splendour about the room as if conscious of their own unchallenged glory. Shakespeare, Keats, Wordsworth, Shelley, Coleridge, Milton, Tennyson, Blake, Browning, Herbert, Cowper, to name only a few all tightly crushed together in the intimacy forced upon them by my personal whims.

I sometimes imagine that when the house is still in the night my books become sentient, aware of their neighbours, approving or disapproving. How, I wonder, does the lofty-minded Wordsworth like being wedged in between Charles Lamb and Ella Wheeler Wilcox? Or how does George Herbert, dear pious soul that he was, react to rubbing shoulders with Lord Byron and Rabindranath Tagore?

If you plunged your hands into a deep casket of precious gems it would not be easy to decide upon which were the most desirable as emeralds, rubies, opals and sapphires slipped through your fingers; nor is it easy to select favourite passages from one's best-loved books; it becomes a process of sifting down to essentials.

The following selections do not represent the sophisticated confectionery of my mental diet; they are the iron rations basic to subsistence. The 103rd Psalm, the Sonnets of Shakespeare and the Odes of Keats are to my mind what daily bread is to the body; a form of nourishment. Though life were stripped to the bone of every other joy these would remain. How could one feel lonely or impoverished in the company of one's most treasured books?

An indefinable sympathy flows between a book and its lover. A book has the capacity to heal and bless even if rarely read. The physical act of holding it in your hand yields its own peculiar delight and by virtue of your love for it over the years you are able to absorb what it has to give of comfort, pleasure or wisdom, according to your need.

For this kind of sensual delight I go chiefly to the shelf that holds the sort of books that were once so easily and cheaply bought in the second-hand book-shops now almost extinct. These shops were usually dark and dusty and a damp musty smell came up at you as you opened the door, but what caves of treasure they were!

I pity the young, for few of them have ever known the bliss of browsing for hours in such places where time ceased to exist, and you could buy exquisitely bound books for less than a shilling. I pity, too, the very young subjected to cranky and compulsory sex education before they are able to quote four lines of

Shakespeare. Much of what is seen on the television screen is a crude assault upon the impressionable wax of a child's fresh mind, turning thoughts inwards instead of outwards to the great world of English literature which is theirs by right of inheritance.

Some of my greatest treasures have been bought for a few coppers. Most of them have gold-edged pages, suéde, leather or morocco covers and charming illustrations. There is a well-worn *Tess of the D'Urbervilles* published in 1891, bound in claret-coloured cloth, priced at sixpence. There is a pocket *Hound of Heaven* by Francis Thompson in a soft green suéde, heavenly to hold and to behold. Eye and hand share in its felicity. From Foyle's, in the Charing Cross Road, came a small book on Watts, bound in a rich crimson leather with lovely reproductions of some of his paintings. This treasure I carried away for the payment of ninepence and in Masons of St Leonards, with its galleries of books, now an ironmongers, I found a first printing of fragments from Jane Austen with a preface by G. K. Chesterton and an interesting set of illustrations dedicated by Jane to Madame la Comtesse De Fevillide. The cover itself is 'a joy forever', plum-coloured with an enchanting design of gold roses and stars circled round a butterfly. This cost me two shillings. Yes, indeed, the good old days. Pity the young.

A delightful feature of the second-hand collection is the inscriptions often to be found on the first leaf. 'To my sailor laddie' 1896. I wonder who he was and what happened to him. 'To Daisy from her Aunt Adelaide'; 'To a much loved Godchild, Emma Corley, Powdermill Cottage, 1901'; 'From Ellen, In gratitude'.

For what? I wonder. They tease the imagination, these ghostly little books which have escaped oblivion by falling into loving hands.

Twelve volumes of Dickens stand stolidly in the space allotted to novels; monumentally impressive, but rarely disturbed, for there is little time now for reading the massive Victorians.

One does not tend to accumulate novels. Most of mine have come to me as gifts, or been acquired by desire. Amongst these are Mary Webb, Trollope, Jane Austen, Ann Bridge, Dostoievsky, Algernon Blackwood, Kate O'Brien and my heart's favourite, Mary Borden. Over and over again I have read *A Woman With White Eyes*, *Jericho Sands*, *Jane Our Stranger* and *Flamingo*. This I consider to be her best. Mary Borden had a great gift for characterisation. As the wife of an M.P. living in Westminster she wrote with the glitter of genius and from personal knowledge of the social side of the political world during the period which followed the end of the First World War. Characters and scenes from *Flamingo* are as real to me today as they were at the time of my first enthralment; the little American, Peter Campbell and his idiot brother the lovable Christopher, Carolina Sal, big Joe's black girl, Frederika Joyce the dispassionate Englishwoman, the beautiful room at Wellowburn with its flamingo screen and the old white house where Peter and Frederika faced with the bitter realisation of their affinity recoiled from a dilemma which was too devastating to be solved within the compass of their circumstances. These people are not for me the evocations of fiction. They are real.

Lovingly I linger over the books which show how

the prophetic promises made to Abraham have been fulfilled. *The Drama of the Lost Disciples*, by G. F. Jowett; *Celt, Druid and Culdee*, by Isabel Hill Elder; *The Stone of Destiny*, by F. Wallace Connon; *Glastonbury*, by P. W. Thompson; *The Tender Twig*, by Francis Henking; and *The Most Valuable Thing in the World*, by W. M. Dodd. It is to these books I turn for inspiration when to outward appearances it would seem that the glory has departed from 'this sceptred isle'. To read the wonderful story of the Coronation Stone is to be injected with a new pride in the great heritage to which I am an heir. To wander in imagination through the ruinous glories of Glastonbury and to drink of the water that flows from the Chalice Well is to recapture the magic of Avalon and to experience a refreshment of vision.

I am not given to introspective moods but there are moments when, looking back over the runaway years, I am reminded of how much and how little I have put into them. It is in such moments of self-questioning that I allow my finger to run along the backs of the fifty-odd smallish books on the Patience Strong shelf which represent the greater part of my working life. For a restoration of confidence I take *Dr Anonymous*[1] out of its place and flick through the pages with a shameless sense of satisfaction for this is the book in which I feel I have justified my existence as a writer. Others could have written a better book, more comprehensive in detail, but none a more loving tribute to Vincent Blumhardt Nesfield, one of the most remarkable men of the century. Browsing through this little

[1] *Doctor Anonymous*, published by Covenant Publishing Co., 6 Buckingham Gate S.W.1.

sketch of a great life I marvel at the fortuitous chain of circumstances that led me to be the one to have the privilege of getting something about 'The Doctor' into print, cursory and inadequate though it was. I never doubted that it was written under the compulsion of Providence for had I put off tackling this important piece of work for even a year it would have been too late and no record would have been left of the life and work of this extraordinary and beloved physician except in the memories of the untold thousands whom he saved from disease, disablement and death.

I cannot complete this brief survey of my treasury without a reference to the twenty-five novels written by my old friend Neil Bell. He was the forerunner of the angry young men, but in his day there really was something to be angry about. Neil Bell was a master of his craft and he achieved success the hard way, teaching in an elementary school by day and writing in the evenings and half the night. Cutting loose from the drudgery of teaching at the age of forty he fled to Cornwall on an impulse, living in one room, with nothing but his pen and his courage. He once spent his last shilling on the postage of a manuscript to his agent. His conversation and his letters were, in my opinion, better than his books, some of which were stridently provocative, but behind all the iconoclastic bluster there was a puckish wit which salted some of the raw realism and redeemed it from crudity. When the political scene is looking drearily hopeless I often dip into the brown paper parcel in which I keep some of the letters he wrote to me during the first great days of our friendship when he was very angry and I was very young, and I enjoy the sort of laugh that makes the stomach muscles ache, a rare treat in these days when nothing is funny any more. Here a memory intrudes of the occasion when Neil Bell introduced me to H. G. Wells at one of Mrs Dawson-Scott's Pen Club dinners. I was eighteen and heavily under the spell of Ann Veronica. The ordinariness of H.G.W.'s appearance had a sobering effect upon my starry-minded romanticism.

When a phrase or a word leaps out at me from the printed page it crystallises into a title. That is why I always think of Shakespeare's 34th sonnet as 'Without My Cloak' and David's 23rd Psalm as 'Green Pastures', words meaning more to me than numbers. The isolating from its text of what I instinctively feel to be an essential thought and to distil it into a title has become a subconscious habit and in gloating over these my chosen treasures I have succumbed to this old temptation.

If I have ventured amongst the immortals with too many personal comments and observations I have merely been fulfilling the purpose behind the writing of this book as suggested by the publishers, not presuming to add word or thought to something which from its conception in the author's mind has been perfect and complete in itself.

CHAPTER TWO

Country Cameos

'The man who is tired of London is tired of life', said Dr Johnson, and 'I was born, as you have heard, in a crowd. This has begot in me an entire affection for that way of life, amounting to an almost insurmountable aversion from solitude and rural scenes', said Charles Lamb, but London is not now what it was in their day. The London sky was not raked by gaunt naked-looking monstrosities of steel and concrete thrusting insolently up above the levels of the old roofs. The streets were not swarming with people, as thick as ants on a nest; the air was not polluted with fumes from the exhausts of cars and buses, and towns had not been allowed to spread beyond the limits of decency.

A child, reared in a small flat in one of those high blocks, is a child deprived of life itself, for lonely it must be up there, with no trees at the window, no people passing by, no street life with its neighbourliness and no garden in which to throw a ball or plant a flower.

A house in a fashionable part of a big city has its cultural compensations but culture is no substitute for life. Suburbanism is another unnatural evil brought about by over-population. Is there any horror like the desolation of miles of detached, semi-detached or terraced houses where few know their neighbours, and as a consequence there is no sense of community except that which forms itself about a church or a chapel.

One can be lonely in the crowds of a city but never in a village or a small market town. There is too much going on: the fêtes, the church bazaars and fellowship centres, the parish councils, the flower shows, the horticultural and dramatic societies, the whist drives, the bridge clubs, the local, and other activities too numerous to mention.

Everybody in the country seems to be busy. There is room to spread yourself, mentally and physically. The air is not used up before the day begins. How can your personality develop without daily contacts with people who share your kind of life?

What is the solution? People must live—so that means more industry, and more industry means more towns. The only answer is to limit the size of families and prohibit immigration, but what Government would have the courage to enforce either?—so many who would prefer to be members of a small community than faceless units in seething masses of humanity must be content to read about the country instead of living in it.

The courtesies of neighbourliness, the graces of good manners, the practice of economy and the hiding of poverty under the proud cloak of courage may have gone with the wind of the Welfare State, but the ladies of Cranford remain, for human nature does not change with a change in social conditions. Miss Matty, Miss Pole, Mrs Jamieson and Lady Glenmire are still with us. The little Cranfordian comedies and dramas are still being played out at the grocer's, the Women's Institute, the church bazaar, the local flower show and, on a somewhat higher level, at the cocktail parties, for Cranford is wherever you can pinpoint a community on a map of rural England.

EVERYBODY'S VILLAGE

Miss Matty and I quietly decided we would have a previous engagement at home: it was on the evening on which Miss Matty usually made candle-lighters of all the notes and letters of the week: for on Mondays her accounts were always made straight—not a penny owing from the week before; so, by a natural arrangement, making candle-lighters fell upon a Tuesday evening, and gave us a legitimate excuse for declining Mrs Jamieson's invitation. But before our answer was written, in came Miss Pole with an open note in her hand.

'So!' she said, 'Ah! I see you have got your note, too. Better late than never. I could have told my Lady Glenmire she would be glad enough of our society before a fortnight was over.'

'Yes', said Miss Matty, 'we're asked for Tuesday evening. And perhaps you would just kindly bring your work across and drink tea with us that night. It is my usual regular time for looking over the last week's bills, and notes, and letters, and making candle-lighters of them; but that does not seem quite reason enough for saying I have a previous engagement at home, though I meant to make it do. Now, if you would come, my conscience would be quite at ease, and luckily the note is not written yet.'

I saw Miss Pole's countenance change while Miss Matty was speaking.

'Don't you mean to go then?' asked she.

'Oh, no!' said Miss Matty quietly. 'You don't either, I suppose?'

'I don't know', replied Miss Pole. 'Yes, I think I do,' said she, rather briskly; and on seeing Miss Matty look surprised, she added, 'You see, one would not like Mrs Jamieson to think that anything she could do, or say, was of consequence enough to give offence; it would be a kind of letting down of ourselves, that I, for one, should not like. It would be too flattering to Mrs Jamieson if we allowed her to suppose that what she had said affected us a week, nay ten days afterwards.'

'Well! I suppose it is wrong to be hurt and annoyed so long about anything; and, perhaps, after all, she did not mean to vex us. But I must say, I could not have brought myself to say the things Mrs Jamieson did about our not calling. I really don't think I shall go.'

'Oh, come! Miss Matty, you must go; you know our friend Mrs Jamieson is much more phlegmatic than most people and does not enter into the little delicacies of feeling which you possess in so remarkable a degree.'

'I thought you possessed them, too, that day Mrs Jamieson called to tell us not to go,' said Miss Matty, innocently.

But Miss Pole, in addition to her delicacies of feeling, possessed a very smart cap, which she was anxious to show to an admiring world; and so she seemed to forget all her angry words uttered not a fortnight before, and to be ready to act on what she called the great Christian principle of 'Forgive and forget'; and she lectured dear Miss Matty so long on this head that she absolutely ended by assuring her it was her duty, as a deceased rector's daughter, to buy a new cap and go to the party at Mrs Jamieson's. So 'we were most happy to accept', instead of 'regretting that we were obliged to decline'.

[From *Cranford*, Chapter 8, by Mrs Gaskell]

THE GREAT WALKERS

[February 23rd, Tuesday, 1802.] A misty rainy morning—the lake calm. I baked bread and pies. Before dinner worked a little at William's waistcoat—after dinner read German grammar. Before tea we walked into Easedale. We turned aside in the Parson's field, a pretty field with three pretty prospects. Then we went to the first large field, but such a cold wind met us that we turned again. The wind seemed warm when we came out of our own door. That dear thrush was singing upon the topmost of the smooth branches of the ash tree at the top of the orchard. How long it had been perched on that same tree I cannot tell, but we had heard its dear voice in the orchard the day through, along with a cheerful undersong made by our winter friends, the robins. We came home by Goan's. I picked up a few mosses by the roadside, which I left at home. We then went to John's Grove, there we sate a little while looking at the fading landscape. The lake, though the objects on the shore were fading, seemed brighter than when it is perfect day, and the Island pushed itself upwards, distinct and large. All the shores marked. There was a sweet sea-like sound in the trees above our heads. We walked backwards and forwards some time for dear John's sake, then walked to look at Rydale. Darkish when we reached home, and we got tea immediately with candles. William now reading in Bishop Hall—I going to read German. We have a nice singing fire, with one piece of wood. Fletcher's carts are arrived but no papers from Mrs Coleridge.

[From Dorothy Wordsworth's *Grasmere Journal*, Volume 1, Edited by E. de Selincourt]

THE HONEYMOON BOUQUET IN THE WINE OF LIFE

Iden liked Mrs Iden to like lavender because his mother had been so fond of it, and all the sixteen carved oak presses which had been so familiar to him in boyhood were full of a thick atmosphere of the plant.

Long since, while yet the honeymoon bouquet remained in the wine of life, Iden had set a hedge of lavender to please his wife. It was so carefully chosen, and set, and watched, that it grew to be the finest lavender in all the country. People used to come for it from round about, quite certain of a favourable reception, for there was nothing so sure to bring peace at Coombe Oaks as a mention of lavender.

But the letter from the Flammas was the great event—from London, all that way, asking for some Coombe Oaks lavender! Then there was billing and cooing, and fraternising, and sunshine in the garden over the hedge of lavender. If only it could have lasted! Somehow, as people grow older there seems so much grating of the wheels.

In time, long time, people's original feelings get strangely confused and overlaid. The church-wardens of the eighteenth century plastered the fresco paintings of the fourteenth in their churches—covered them up with yellowish mortar. The mould grows up, and hides the capital of the fallen column, the acanthus is hidden in earth. At the foot of the oak, where it is oldest, the bark becomes dense and thick, impenetrable, and without sensitiveness; you may cut off an inch thick without reaching the sap. A sort of scale or caking in long, long time grows over original feelings.

[From *Amaryllis at the Fair*, Chapter 9, by Richard Jefferies (1848–87)]

A LETTER FROM SELBORNE, APRIL 12th, 1770

Dear Sir,—I heard many birds of several species sing last year after Midsummer, enough to prove that the summer solstice is not the period that puts a stop to the music of the woods. The yellow-hammer no doubt persists with more steadiness than any other: but the woodlark, the wren, the redbreast, the swallow, the whitethroat, the goldfinch, the common linnet, are all undoubted instances of the truth of what I advanced.

If this severe season does not interrupt the regularity of the summer migrations, the black-cap will be here in two or three days. I wish it was in my power to procure you one of those songsters; but I am no bird-catcher, and so little used to birds in a cage, that I fear if I had one it would soon die for want of skill in feeding.

[From *Natural History of Selborne*, by Gilbert White (1720–93)]

LIVING LAWN-MOWERS ON THE SUSSEX DOWNS

These blossoming places in the wilderness which I have tried to describe, and which make the thought of our trim, pretty artificial gardens a weariness, are not too many: in most places the untilled downs are bare of furze and bramble and the plants that take advantage of the bramble's protection are close-cropped by the sheep. Their very smoothness gives them a character which is quite unique and has a peculiar charm. Flowers are abundant and in considerable variety but many that are luxuriant in rich soils wherever there is shelter and protection, here scarcely look like the same species: they have changed their habits of growth, their form and size, to suit the different conditions. The luxury of long stems, the delight of waving in the wind, and the ambition to overtop their neighbours, would here be fatal. Their safety lies in nestling down amid the lowly grass, keeping so close to the earth as to be able to blossom and ripen their seed in spite of the ever-nibbling sheep—the living lawn-mowers perpetually moving over them.

[From *Nature in Downland*, Chapter 3, by W. H. Hudson (1841–1922)]

YOU AND YOUR SHADOW

In a green, over-bowered lane, where the birds shake dew and blossoms from the hedgerows, and spots of sun chequer the wayside grass, look for your own shadow. At what hour is it behind? When the sun shines in your face, your shadow is at your back. And has it ever been otherwise with poet, painter, or man of noble thought and magnificent enterprise? with Milton? or Columbus? Long and wearisome is their road to glory; steep and entangled is the path towards the rising orb of fame. They behold not the shadow which they cast; it stretches after them—cheering others, not themselves.

Retrace your steps down the glimmering lane. Let it be evening. What a change! Warm streaks of light gild the edges of bird-homes, and sleep in the dim hollows of mossy oaks. Where is your shadow now? It has sprung twenty feet before you, as if it were rushing up the garden, to sit down in the parlour, before you can turn the corner. It is a race between you and your shadow; but you will never overtake it while you travel from the sun. Can you make no simile out of this? When the day of intellectual life sets, and the pilgrim of poetry, eloquence, or art walks away from the glory of the morning, where is his shadow? It is thrown forward into the untrodden paths of the future, and lengthens at every step, into the rich orchards of a remoter or sunnier climate.

The shadow gives a parallel for a life as well as for a genius. That man fleeth like a shadow and never continueth in one stay, is among the most touching lessons of the dead.

I am pleased to trace out the resemblance in my summer rambles; and when I see myself climbing the silver beech, and losing my head in the top branches, a moral is not wanting.... I remember with good Arthur Warwick, that all our pleasures are shadows, thrown by prosperous sunlight along our journey, and ever deceiving and flying us most when most we follow them. The vapoury form on the mossy pales, with the robin singing over its head, is only the emblem of some empty dream that walks through life by our side, with hope carolling above it, and disappearing when reflection draws near, and looks at it with calm and earnest eye. But, while I moralize, the sun is sinking fast.

[From *Summer Time in the Country*, by the Revd R. A. Willmott; published in 1858 with illustrations from drawings by Birket Foster]

THE LADY-LOOK

Next to his house, though parted from it by another long garden with a yew arbour at the end, is the pretty dwelling of the shoemaker, a pale, sickly-looking, black-haired man, the very model of sober industry.

There he sits in his little shop from early morning till late at night. An earthquake would hardly stir him: the illumination did not. He stuck immoveably to his last, from the first lighting up, through the long blaze and the slow decay till his large solitary candle was the only light in the place. One cannot conceive anything more perfect than the contempt which the man of transparencies and the man of shoes must have felt for each other on that evening. There was at least as much vanity in the sturdy industry as in the strenuous idleness, for our shoemaker is a man of substance, he employs three journeymen, two lame, and one a dwarf, so that his shop looks like an hospital; he has purchased the lease of his commodious dwelling, some even say that he has bought it out and out; and he has only one pretty daughter, a light, delicate, fair-haired girl of fourteen, the champion, protectress, and playfellow of every brat under three years old, whom she jumps, dances, dandles, and feeds all day long. A very attractive person is that child-loving girl. I have never seen anyone in her station who possessed so thoroughly that undefinable charm, the lady-look. See her on a Sunday in her simplicity and her white frock, and she might pass for an earl's daughter. She likes flowers too, and has a profusion of white stocks under her window, as pure and delicate as herself.

[From *Our Village*, by Mary Russell Mitford (1787–1855)]

LOVED FOR ITS OWN SAKE

'I feel that the loss of the love of the land for its own sake and the loss of the Christian religion are the greatest tragedies this country has ever suffered'. This is an extract from a letter written during the 2nd World War by a naval lieutenant to that great nature-lover and author, the late H. J. Massingham. Those words inspired him to write one of the best of his books, *The Tree of Life*. Thirty years after Massingham we have a soil contamination problem on our hands. A farmer should be a philosopher before he is a government servant or a cash-conscious businessman. To retain its health and be able to fulfil the purpose for which the good Lord created it land must be treated with reverence; as the lieutenant said, 'loved for its own sake'. Manufacturers of chemical fertilisers, please note.

LET PHYSICIANS PRATE

ANEMONE . . . Called also Wind-flower, because they say that the flowers never open except when the wind bloweth. Pliny is my author; if it be not so, blame him. The seed also, if it bears any at all, flies away with the wind.

PLACE AND TIME.—They are sown usually in the gardens of the curious, and flower in the spring-time. As for description, I shall pass it, being well known to all those that sow them.

GOVERNMENT AND VIRTUES.—It is under the dominion of Mars, being supposed to be a kind of crow's-foot. The leaves provoke the terms mightily, being boiled, and the decoction drank. The body being bathed with the decoction of them, cures the leprosy: the leaves being stamped, and the juice snuffed up the nose, purgeth the head mightily; so doth the root, being chewed in the mouth, for it procureth much spitting, and bringeth away many watery and phlegmatic humours, and is therefore excellent for the lethargy. And when all is done, let physicians prate what they please, all the pills in the dispensary purge not the head like to hot things held in the mouth. Being made into an ointment, and the eyelids anointed with it, it helps inflammations of the eyes; whereby it is palpable, that every stronger draweth its weaker like. The same ointment is excellent good to cleanse malignant and corroding ulcers.

[From *Culpeper's Herbal* (Astrologer-physician, 1616–54)]

THE PARTING SHOT

'May God forgive you, madam, for the manner in which you have treated me', said Mr Slope, looking at her with a very heavenly look; 'and remember this, madam, that you yourself may still have a fall;' and he looked at her with a very worldly look. 'As to the bishop, I pity him! And so saying, Mr Slope left the room. Thus ended the intimacy of the Bishop of Barchester with his first confidential chaplain.

Mrs Proudie was right in this; namely, that Mr Slope was not insane enough to publish to the world any of his doings in Barchester. He did not trouble his friend Mr Towers with any written statement of the iniquity of Mrs Proudie, or the imbecility of her husband. He was aware that it would be wise in him to drop for the future all allusions to his doings in the cathedral city. Soon after the interview just recorded he left Barchester, shaking the dust off his feet as he entered the railway carriage; and he gave no longing lingering look after the cathedral towers, as the train hurried him quickly out of their sight.

It is well known that the family of the Slopes never starve: they always fall on their feet like cats, and let them fall where they will, they live on the fat of the land. Our Mr Slope did so. On his return to town he found that the sugar refiner had died, and that his widow was inconsolable; or, in other words, in want of consolation. Mr Slope consoled her, and soon found himself settled with much comfort in the house in Baker Street. He possessed himself, also, before long, of a church in the vicinity of the New Road, and became known to fame as one of the most eloquent preachers and pious clergymen in that part of the metropolis. There let us leave him.

Of the bishop and his wife very little further need be said. From that time forth nothing material occurred to interrupt the even course of their domestic harmony. Very speedily, a further vacancy on the bench of bishops gave to Dr Proudie the seat in the House of Lords, which he at first so anxiously longed for. But by this time he had become a wiser man. He did certainly take his seat, and occasionally registered a vote in favour of government views on ecclesiastical matters. But he had thoroughly learnt that his proper sphere of action lay in close contiguity with Mrs Proudie's wardrobe. He never again aspired to disobey, or seemed even to wish for autocratic diocesan authority. If ever he thought of freedom he did so as men think of the millennium, as of a good time which may be coming, but which nobody expects to come in their day. Mrs Proudie might be said still to bloom and was, at any rate, strong; and the bishop had no reason to apprehend that he would be speedily visited with the sorrows of a widower's life.

He is still Bishop of Barchester. He has so graced that throne, that the government has been averse to translate him, even to higher dignities. There may he remain, under safe pupilage, till the new-fangled manners of the age have discovered him to be superannuated, and bestowed on him a pension. As for Mrs Proudie, our prayers for her are that she may live forever.

[From *Barchester Towers*, Chapter 51, by Anthony Trollope (1851–82)]

A CORE OF SWEETNESS

The attic was close under the thatch, and there were many nests beneath the eaves, and a continual twittering of swallows. The attic window was in a big gable, and the roof on one side went right down to the ground, with a tall chimney standing up above the roof-tree. Somewhere among the beams of the attic was a wild bees' nest, and you could hear them making a sleepy soft murmuring and morning and evening you could watch them going in a line to the mere for water, so, it being very still there, with the fair shadows of the apple trees peopling the orchard outside, that was void, as were the near meadows, Gideon being in the far field making hay-cocks, which I also should have been doing, there came to me, I cannot tell whence, a most powerful sweetness that had never come to me afore. It was not religious, like the goodness of a text heard at a preaching. It was beyond that. It was as if some creature made all of light had come on a sudden from a great way off, and nestled in my bosom. On all things there came a fair, lovely look, as if a different air stood over them. It is a look that seems ready to come sometimes on those gleamy mornings after rain, when they say, 'So fair the day, the cuckoo is going to heaven'.

Only this was not of the day, but of summat beyond it. I cared not to ask what it was. For when the nut-hatch comes into her own tree, she dunna ask who planted it, nor what name it bears to men. For the tree is all to the nut-hatch, and this was all to me. Afterwards, when I had mastered the reading of the book, I read

His banner over me was love.

And it called to mind that evening. But if you should have said 'Whose banner?' I couldna have answered. And even now, when Parson says, 'It was the power of the Lord working in you,' I'm not sure in my own mind. For there was nought in it of churches or of folks, praying nor praising, sinning nor repenting. It had to do with such things as bird-song and daffadowndillies rustling, knocking their heads together in the wind. And it was as wilful in its coming and going as a breeze over the standing corn. It was a queer thing, too, that a woman who spent her days in sacking, cleaning sties and beast-housen, living hard, considering over fardens, should come of a sudden upon such a marvel as this. For though it was so quiet, it was a great miracle, and it changed my life; for when I was lost for something to turn to, I'd run to the attic, and it was a core of sweetness in much bitter.

[From *Precious Bane*, Chapter 7,
by Mary Webb (1881–1927)]

THE HAPPINESS OF A COUNTRY FIRESIDE

Thus runs the heading for Chapter VI of *The Vicar of Wakefield*, but I wonder if the Vicar's daughters would have thought that happiness was the right word when they saw Father, poker in hand, have that unfortunate accident with their carefully prepared complexion lotion.

As we expected our landlord the next day, my wife went to make the venison pasty. Moses sat reading, while I taught the little ones; my daughters seemed equally busy with the rest; and I observed them for a good while cooking something over the fire. I at first supposed that they were assisting their mother, but little Dick informed me in a whisper, that they were making a wash for the face. Washes of all kinds I had a natural antipathy to; for I knew that instead of mending the complexion they spoiled it. I therefore approached my chair by sly degrees to the fire, and grasping the poker, as if it wanted mending, seemingly by accident, overturned the whole composition, and it was too late to begin another.

[Oliver Goldsmith (1728–74)]

IN EACH OTHER'S WAY

Society is commonly too cheap. We meet at very short intervals, not having had time to acquire any new value for each other. We meet at meals three times a day, and give each other a new taste of that old musty cheese that we are. We have had to agree on a certain set of rules, called etiquette and politeness, to make this frequent meeting tolerable and that we need not come to open war. We meet at the post-office, and at the sociable, and about the fireside every night; we live thick and are in each other's way and stumble over one another, and I think that we thus lose some respect for one another. Certainly less frequency would suffice for all important and hearty communications. Consider the girls in a factory—never alone, hardly in their dreams. It would be better if there were but one inhabitant to a square mile, as where I live. The value of a man is not in his skin, that we should touch him.

I have a great deal of company in my house; especially in the morning, when nobody calls.'

[From *Walden*, by Henry David Thoreau (1817–62)]

Christmas is wherever you happen to be, but to get the real feel of it you must be where, on your way to midnight communion on Christmas Eve, you will pass a lamplit stable by the yard of an inn and pretend that it is Bethlehem. You must be where it is quiet enough to hear the bells across the fields and where, after you have eaten your locally reared turkey, you can make your merriment by a fire of logs cut from a near-by wood. It is odd that, for me, the magic of Christmas in the English countryside has been captured, not by an Englishman, but by an American, for Christmas would not be complete without a passing peep into the windows of Bracebridge Hall.

ON CHRISTMAS DAY IN THE MORNING

When I woke the next morning, it seemed as if all the events of the preceding evening had been a dream, and nothing but the identity of the ancient chamber convinced me of their reality. While I lay musing on my pillow, I heard the sound of little feet pattering outside of the door, and a whispering consultation. Presently a choir of small voices chanted forth an old Christmas carol, the burden of which was—

> Rejoice, our Saviour he was born
> On Christmas day in the morning.

I rose softly, slipped on my clothes, opened the door suddenly, and beheld one of the most beautiful little fairy groups that a painter could imagine. It consisted of a boy and two girls, the eldest not more than six, and lovely as seraphs. They were going the rounds of the house, and singing at every chamber door; but my sudden appearance frightened them into mute bashfulness. They remained for a moment playing on their lips with their fingers, and now and then stealing a shy glance, from under their eyebrows, until, as if by one impulse, they scampered away, and as they turned an angle of the gallery, I heard them laughing in triumph at their escape.

Everything conspired to produce kind and happy feelings in this stronghold of old-fashioned hospitality. The window of my chamber looked out upon what in summer would have been a beautiful landscape. There was a sloping lawn, a fine stream winding at the foot of it, and a tract of park beyond, with noble clumps of trees, and herds of deer. At a distance was a neat hamlet, with the smoke from the cottage chimneys hanging over it; and a church with its dark spire in strong relief against the clear cold sky. The house was surrounded with evergreens, according to the English custom, which would have given almost an appearance of summer; but the morning was extremely frosty; the light vapour of the preceding evening had been precipitated by the cold, and covered all the trees and every blade of grass with its fine crystallisations. The rays of a bright morning sun had a dazzling effect among the glittering foliage. A robin, perched upon the top of a mountain ash that hung its clusters of red berries just before my window, was basking himself in the sunshine, and piping a few querulous notes; and a peacock was displaying all the glories of his train, and strutting with the pride and gravity of a Spanish grandee, on the terrace walk below.

I had scarcely dressed myself, when a servant appeared to invite me to family prayers. He showed me the way to a small chapel in the old wing of the house, where I found the principal part of the family already assembled in a kind of gallery, furnished with cushions, hassocks, and large prayer-books; the servants were seated on benches below. The old gentleman read prayers from a desk in front of the gallery, and Master Simon acted as clerk, and made the responses; and I must do him the justice to say that he acquitted himself with great gravity and decorum.

[*The Keeping of Christmas at Bracebridge Hall*, by Washington Irving (1783–1859)]

CHAPTER THREE

Shakespeare's Casket

Could it be a mere freak of coincidence that Shakespeare was born on St George's Day, the Patron Saint of England? Shakespeare *is* England. Moving amongst the varied nationalities that swarm around the streets of little Stratford throughout the year you feel it would be nearer to the truth to say that Shakespeare is more than England; he is the world. Keats's reverence for Shakespeare was expressed in a marginal note in a folio copy of the plays. 'The genius of Shakespeare', wrote Keats, 'was an innate universality; wherefore he laid the achievements of human intellect prostrate beneath his indolent and kingly gaze; he could do easily men's utmost.' That last phrase hits the mark. The writing of a play which would have stretched a better-educated man to the full limit of his physical and mental capacity would have come easily to Will Shakespeare. If he had had to sweat blood over his work in London he would never have survived to enjoy a comfortable retirement in his home town. Son of a middle-class glover and scholar at the local grammar school he never needed the gloss of an expensive education because he knew it all without teacher or tutor.

The Greeks had their playwrights before Christ walked in Galilee, but out of the brain of Shakespeare came not only tragic figures like Lear and Coriolanus but elves, ghosts, jesters, witches and fairies. He knew all there was to know about the burdens of kingship, the art of war and the craft of politics, but he also knew about violets, primroses, rosemary and rue. He knew that daffodils come 'before the swallow dares' for he was a country boy familiar with the orchards of Shottery, the mill at Welford, the oaks of Charlecote and the Avonside meadows before he ever saw the streets of London or the inside of an Elizabethan theatre.

In my early days I was lucky to have lived in localities within easy reach of the Old Vic, usually no more than a twopenny tram ride. Parties of schoolchildren were taken from all parts of London to performances given by the Ben Greet Players and, if I remember rightly, the Frank Benson companies. Most of us could recite from memory the main speeches in *A Midsummer Night's Dream* and *The Merchant of Venice* before we knew how we were born. Had such knowledge been available I do not think it would have roused much interest, for how much room would be left over for such a subject in minds dizzy with the flitterings of Titania's attendants and the heady oratory of Brutus?

Shakespeare holds up a mirror to human nature which reflects the red-in-tooth-and-claw ruthlessness of Lady Macbeth, the malice of Iago, the shilly-shallying irresolution of Hamlet and all the foibles and vanities of the characters that crowd the Shakespearian stage, and in this same mirror we see ourselves, what we might become, what we might have been and what we are.

Deep is the casket and rich the contents, but for my

first choice I cannot but seize upon the many-faceted jewel of Hamlet's vacillating but sublime soliloquy.

The points of Hamlet's self-questionings probe at nerves that lie near to the surface of every man's skin.

What's to be done? Are we to watch the oncoming tides of misfortune in submissive silence or do we get up and push back the waves? Is there any real escape from life? Who can tell? What traveller has ever returned from the unseen and undiscovered country of death? The pricks or the bludgeonings of conscience make cowards of the bravest. It is not possible for a man to know exactly where he is going or why. The firmest decision can be turned in its direction by an unexpected cross-current of circumstances.

NO TRAVELLER RETURNS

To be, or not to be,—that is the question:—
Whether 'tis nobler in the mind to suffer the slings
And arrows of outrageous fortune, or to take arms against
A sea of troubles, and by opposing end them?—
To die,—to sleep,—No more; and by a sleep to say we end
The heart-ache and the thousand natural shocks
That flesh is heir to,—'tis a consummation
Devoutly to be wish'd. To die,—to sleep,—
To sleep! perchance to dream:—ay there's the rub;
For in that sleep of death what dreams may come,
When we have shuffled off this mortal coil,
Must give us pause: there's the respect
That makes calamity of so long life;
For who would bear the whips and scorns of time,
The oppressor's wrong, the proud man's contumely,
The pangs of dispriz'd love, the law's delay
The insolence of office, and the spurns
That patient merit of the unworthy takes,
When he himself might his quietus make
With a bare bodkin? who would fardels bear,
To grunt and sweat under a weary life,
But that the dread of something after death,—
The undiscover'd country, from whose bourn
No traveller returns,—
Than fly to others that we know not of?
Thus conscience does make cowards of us all;
And thus the native hue of resolution
Is sicklied o'er with the pale cast of thought;
And enterprises of great pith and moment,
With this regard, their currents turn awry,
And lose the name of action.—Soft you now!
The fair Ophelia.—Nymph, in thy orisons
Be all my sins remember'd.

[*Hamlet*, Act III, Scene 1]

WHEN MERCY SEASONS JUSTICE

The quality of mercy is not strain'd;
It droppeth as the gentle rain from heaven
Upon the place beneath: it is twice bless'd
It blesseth him that gives and him that takes:
'Tis mightiest in the mightiest; it becomes
The throned monarch better than his crown;
His sceptre shows the force of temporal power,
The attribute to awe and majesty,
Wherein doth sit the dread and fear of kings;
But mercy is above this sceptr'd sway—
It is enthronéd in the heart of kings,
It is an attribute to God himself;
And earthly power doth then show likest God's
When mercy seasons justice. Therefore Jew,
Though justice be thy plea consider this—
That in the course of justice none of us
Should see salvation: we do pray for mercy;
And that same prayer doth teach us all to render
The deeds of mercy.

[From *The Merchant of Venice*, Act IV, Scene 1]

Into the Venetian Court where Shylock's claim against Antonio was being fought out within the clearly defined terms of the law with hard talk about ducats and bonds came Portia with soft talk about God, heaven and the gentle rain of mercy and suddenly the whole sordid business was lifted out of the context of justice and presented as an ethical and religious issue, for the mercy speech was surely one of the loveliest sermons ever written or preached; and yet I have never felt able to indict Shylock for being unmoved by it. Shylock most probably would never even have heard of the 5th beatitude so the Christians had the advantage over him there. And in the end Antonio was saved by virtue of the strict letter of the law, not by the beautifully worded appeal of the sharp-witted and high-minded Portia. Not that the rightness of her argument could be questioned, for as she truly says, none of us would see salvation if justice took its course.

THE SINGING STARS

How sweet the moonlight sleeps upon this bank!
Here we will sit and let the sounds of music
Creep in our ears; soft stillness and the night
Becomes the touches of sweet harmony.
Sit Jessica. Look how the floor of heaven
Is thick inlaid with patines of bright gold;
There's not the smallest orb which thou behold'st
But in his motion like an angel sings,
Still quiring to the young ey'd cherubims:
Such harmony is in immortal souls;
But whilst this muddy vesture of decay
Doth grossly close it in, we cannot hear it.

[From *The Merchant of Venice*, Act V, Scene 1]

These words of Lorenzo to Shylock's daughter Jessica are as full of sweetness as a hive with honey. Who but Shakespeare could have pictured the floor of heaven being 'inlaid with patines of bright gold' or thought of the stars as singing like angels? They diffuse a dreamy sensuousness that drugs the mind, for under the hypnotic influence of their beauty we are lost to reality and transported into a world where two imaginary lovers sit on a moonlit bank listening to the music of the stars.

Such is the potency of the Shakespearian magic.

Polonius gave sound advice to his son when he gave him his blessing. The farewell speech to Laertes is peppered with maxims which have become common currency in the English language and are still valid, for moral truths do not change with the changing times.

'Neither a borrower nor a lender be', said wise old Polonius. In lending you are likely to lose not only your money but your friend and if you have a good friend, he said, one whose love and loyalty have been tested in the fires of experience, 'grapple him to your soul with hoops of steel'. Do not go chasing after every new acquaintance. Dress according to your means and not according to your fancy. Accept criticism, but reserve judgment. Think before you go plunging into a quarrel. And above all, never let down your own standards. In brief, be true to yourself.

THIS ABOVE ALL

Yet here, Laertes! aboard, aboard, for the wind sits
In the shoulder of your sail,
And you are stay'd for. There,—my blessing with you!
And these few precepts in thy memory
Look thou character. Give thy thoughts no tongue,
Nor any unproportion'd thought his act.
Be thou familiar, but by no means vulgar.
The friends thou hast, and their adoption tried,
Grapple them to thy soul with hoops of steel;
But do not dull thy palm with entertainment
Of each new-hatch'd, unfledg'd comrade. Beware
Of entrance to a quarrel; but, being in,
Bear't that the opposed may beware of thee.
Give every man thine ear, but few thy voice:
Take each man's censure, but reserve thy judgment.
Costly thy habit as thy purse can buy,
But not express'd in fancy; rich, not gaudy:
For the apparel oft proclaims the man;
And they in France of the best rank and station
Are most select and generous chief in that.
Neither a borrower nor a lender be:
For loan oft loses both itself and friend;
And borrowing dulls the edge of husbandry.
This above all—to thine own self be true;
And it must follow, as the night the day,
Thou canst not then be false to any man.
Farewell: my blessing season this in thee!

[*Hamlet*, Act III, Scene 1]

BEFORE HARFLEUR AND AFTER DUNKIRK

Once more unto the breach, dear friends, once more;
Or close the wall up with our English dead!
In peace there's nothing so becomes a man
As modest stillness and humility:
But when the blast of war blows in our ears,
Then imitate the action of the tiger;
Stiffen the sinews, summon up the blood,
Disguise fair nature with hard-favour'd rage;
Then lend the eye a terrible aspect;
Let it pry through the portage of the head
Like the brass cannon; let the brow o'erwhelm it
As fearfully as doth a galled rock
O'erhang and jutty his confounded base,
Swill'd with the wild and wasteful ocean,
Now set the teeth and stretch the nostril wide;
Hold hard the breath and bend up every spirit
To his full height!—On, on you noblest English,
Whose blood is fet from fathers of war-proof!—
Fathers that, like so many Alexanders,
Have in these parts from morn till even fought,
And sheath'd their swords for lack of argument:—
Dishonour not your mothers; now attest
That those whom you call'd fathers did beget you!
Be copy now to men of grosser blood,
And teach them how to war! And you, good yeomen,
Whose limbs were made in England, show us here
The mettle of your pasture, let us swear
That you are worth your breeding, which I doubt not;
For there is none of you so mean and base,
That hath not noble lustre in your eyes.
I see you stand like greyhounds in the slips,
Straining upon the start. The game's afoot:
Follow your spirit; and upon this charge
Cry—God for Harry! England! and Saint George!

[*Henry V*, Act III, Scene 1]

Churchill, making his famous 1940 speeches at a time when Britain stood alone against the Germans, having been abandoned and betrayed by her continental allies, was saying what Henry V said at Harfleur and in the same spirit. For us, as for Henry, there was nothing left but a grim choice between two lines of action: to attack or to close up the breach with our English dead. For both men capitulation would have been unthinkable.

And in the grim waiting days of 1943–44, when all along the creeks and crevices of our coasts boats and planes were being mustered secretly for the final onslaught of D Day, we too were standing in the slips, 'straining upon the start'. Hold hard the breath and bend up every spirit to his full height. So spoke Henry V of England and so spoke Winston Churchill. And this is precisely what we did. Had we done less this little island of ours would have gone down under the obscene tyranny of Hitler and ceased to be the 'demi-paradise' of Shakespeare's free England.

THE FORGERIES OF JEALOUSY

These are the forgeries of jealousy:
And never, since the middle summer's spring,
Met we on hill, in dale, forest, or mead,
By pavéd fountain, or by rushy brook,
Or on the beachéd margent of the sea,
To dance our ringlets to the whistling wind,
But with thy brawls thou hast disturb'd our sport.
Therefore the winds, piping to us in vain,
As in revenge, have suck'd up from the sea
Contagious fogs; which falling in the land,
Have every pelting river made so proud
That they have overborne their continents:
The ox hath therefore stretch'd his yoke in vain,
The ploughman lost his sweat; and the green corn
Hath rotted ere his youth attain'd a beard:

The fold stands empty in the drowned field,
And crows are fatted with the murrain flock;
The nine men's morris is fill'd up with mud;
And the quaint mazes in the wanton green,
For lack of tread, are undistinguishable:
The human mortals want their winter here;
No night is now with hymn or carol blest:
Therefore the moon, the governess of floods,
Pale in her anger, washes all the air,
That rheumatic diseases do abound:
And thorough this distemperature we see
The seasons alter: hoary-headed frosts
Fall in the fresh lap of the crimson rose;
And on old Hyem's chin and icy crown
An odorous chaplet of sweet summer buds
Is, as in mockery, set: the spring, the summer,
The childing autumn, angry winter, change
Their wonted liveries; and the mazé'd world,
By their increase, now knows not which is which:
And this same progeny of evils comes
From our debate, from our dissension:
We are their parents and original.

[From *A Midsummer Night's Dream*, Act II, Scene 2]

Did ever wife berate a husband in such felicitous language? In making her point against the jealous and acquisitive Oberon Titania clothes invective in poetry and softens the force of argument. The employment of such phrases as 'hoary-headed frosts fall in the fresh lap of the crimson rose' and 'an odorous chaplet of sweet summer buds' must surely weaken the case of the haranguer. Small wonder that this recitation of his malicious acts fell on the truculent Oberon like water on a duck's back.

THE LANGUAGE OF LOVE

He jests at scars that never felt a wound.—
But, soft! what light through yonder window breaks?

It is the east, and Juliet is the sun!—
Arise, fair sun, and kill the envious moon,
Who is already sick and pale with grief,
That thou her maid art far more fair than she:
Her vestal livery is but sick and green,
And none but fools do wear it; cast it off.—
It is my lady; O, it is my love!
O, that she knew she were!—
She speaks, yet she says nothing: what of that?
Her eye discourses, I will answer it.—
I am too bold, 'tis not to me she speaks:
Two of the fairest stars in all the heaven,
Having some business do entreat her eyes
To twinkle in their spheres till they return.
What if her eyes were there, they in her head?
The brightness of her cheek would shame those stars,
As daylight doth a lamp; her eyes in heaven
Would through the airy region stream so bright
That birds would sing, and think it were not night.—
See how she leans her cheek upon her hand!
O, that I were a glove upon that hand,
That I might touch that cheek!

[*Romeo and Juliet*, Act II, Scene 2]

Whatever happened to romance? Somehow it seems to have been washed away down the kitchen sink of the self-indulgent society with a lot of other lovely things like reticence, sentiment, modesty and chastity. Frankness of speech on sexual matters in public and private has stripped love of its mysteries and youth of its dreams. Pity the Romeos and Juliets of this crude age who know all the biological answers and yet are immature, knowing nothing of the pangs and raptures of romantic love!

THIS ENGLAND

This royal throne of kings, this sceptr'd isle
This earth of majesty, this seat of Mars,

This other Eden, demi-paradise;
This fortress built by Nature for herself
Against infection and the hand of war;
This happy breed of men, this little world;
This precious stone set in the silver sea,
Which serves it in the office of a wall,
Or as a moat defensive to a house,
Against the envy of less happier lands;
This blessed plot, this earth, this realm, this England,
This nurse, this teeming womb of royal kings,
Fear'd by their breed, and famous by their birth,
Renowned for their deeds as far from home,—
For Christian service and true chivalry,—
As is the sepulchre in stubborn Jewry
Of the world's ransom, blessed Mary's Son;—
This land of such dear souls, this dear dear land,
Dear for her reputation through the world,
Is now leas'd out—I die, pronouncing it,—
Like to a tenement or pelting farm:
England, bound in with the triumphant sea,
Whose rocky shore beats back the envious siege
Of watery Neptune, is now bound in with shame,
With inky blots, and rotten parchment bonds:
That England, that was wont to conquer others,
Hath made a shameful conquest of itself.
Ah, would the scandal vanish with my life,
How happy then were my ensuing death!

[*King Richard II*, Act II, Scene 1]

When a politician tells me that I am a European I reach for my Shakespeare and read the John of Gaunt speech from Act II, Sc. 1 of *Richard II*. This I do to take the heat out of my indignation, not for reassurance; for I need no confirmation of the self-evident fact that Britain, mother of a family of nations, has been able to fulfil her unique destiny in the world only by reason of the fact that she has been separated from the Continent by 'the triumphant sea'. We are a people set apart from the Latin countries not only by geography but by differences in blood and breed. In the very marrow of my Anglo-Saxon bones I know it to be true, and no matter how many politicians may assert that the signing away of our birthright would be good for business the majority believe that it is upon the resources of our own Commonwealth that we should base our economic policies.

When Shakespeare wrote of the sea as a 'defensive moat' he little dreamed days would come when it would be our only protection. Or did he? Julius Caesar attempted it before Christ was born and being out-fought by the Britons had to retire to lick his wounds. The dreams of Phillip of Spain, Napoleon of France, Kaiser William of Prussia and Adolf Hitler of Austria all foundered on the rocks of our guardian cliffs.

The closing lines of the John of Gaunt speech seem to have a prophetic significance in the context of our present situation when the fate of 'this other Eden' hangs in the balance, especially in the reference to England making a shameful conquest of herself and of 'inky blots'. Could there have been some kind of pre-vision of that fateful day in Brussels when, before signing the Treaty of Accession, the Prime Minister was bespattered with 'inky blots'?

Let the Channel Tunnel enthusiasts read what Shakespeare put into the mouth of John of Gaunt when he spoke of 'this precious stone set in the silver sea', and, please God, may they get the message.

'AND SORROWS END'

When to the sessions of sweet silent thought
I summon up remembrance of things past,
I sigh the lack of many a thing I sought,
And with old woes new wail my dear times' waste:
Then can I drown an eye, unus'd to flow,
For precious friends hid in death's dateless night,
And weep afresh love's long-since cancell'd woe,
And moan the expense of many a vanish'd sight.

Then can I grieve at grievances foregone,
And heavily from woe to woe tell o'er
The sad account of fore-bemoaned moan,
Which I new pay as if not paid before.
But if the while I think on thee, dear friend,
All losses are restor'd, and sorrows end.

[Sonnet 30]

THE DARLING BUDS OF MAY

Shall I compare thee to a summer's day?
Thou are more lovely and more temperate:
Rough winds do shake the darling buds of May,
And summer's lease hath all too short a date:
Sometime too hot the eye of heaven shines,
And often is his gold complexion dimm'd;
And every fair from fair sometime declines,
By chance, or nature's changing course, untrimm'd;
But thy eternal summer shall not fade,
Nor lose possession of that fair thou owest;
Nor shall Death brag thou wander'st in his shade,
When in eternal lines to time thou growest;
So long as men can breathe, or eyes can see,
So long lives this, and this gives life to thee.

[Sonnet 18]

SO TRUE A FOOL IS LOVE

Being your slave, what should I do but tend
Upon the hours and times of your desire?
I have no precious time at all to spend,
Nor services to do, till you require.
Nor date I chide the world-without-end hour,
Whilst I, my sovereign, watch the clock for you,
Nor think the bitterness of absence sour,
When you have bid your servant once adieu;
Nor dare I question with my jealous thought
Where you may be, or your affairs suppose,
But, like a sad slave, stay and think of nought
Save, where you are, how happy you make those:

So true a fool is love, that in your will
(Though you do anything) he thinks no ill.

[Sonnet 57]

WITHOUT MY CLOAK

Why didst thou promise such a beauteous day,
And make me travel forth without my cloak,
To let base clouds o'ertake me in my way,
Hiding thy bravery in their rotten smoke?
'Tis not enough that through the cloud thou break,
To dry the rain on my storm-beaten face,
For no man well of such a salve can speak,
That heals the wound, and cures not the disgrace:
Nor can thy shame give physic to my grief;
Though thou repent, yet I have still the loss:
The offender's sorrow lends but weak relief
To him that bears the strong offence's cross,
Ah! but those tears are pearl which thy love sheds,
And they are rich, and ransom all ill deeds.

[Sonnet 34]

These are but four of the one hundred and fifty-four gems in the jewel box of the Shakespearean sonnets. Much as I love the 18th with its 'summer's lease hath all too short a date' and the sublime 30th with its 'sessions of sweet silent thought' it is to the 34th that I turn when unlooked-for calamity dashes some dazzling hope and makes wreckage of a dream. It is then that I am tempted to vent my frustration upon the good Lord, questioning why He should have allowed me to venture out into the capricious sunshine of life with such a gay confidence in myself, only to be beaten back ignominiously by a freak storm; caught out in the rain with no protective cloak to cover my humiliation.

CHAPTER FOUR

A Rosary of Prayers

The fundamental urge for man to communicate with something beyond himself is as deep an instinct as the instinct to love, to live, to eat and to survive. Even to the unbeliever there come moments in life when he wishes he could pray, and heart desires what lips deny.

The Greeks and the Romans made their own gods and prayed to them, but Israel was a theocracy from the beginning, for the history of Israel is the history of their worship of and involvement with the one invisible God. Monotheism began in Eden. Out of the hard soil of Judaism flowered the glory of Christianity with its new covenant and its new way of praying, for after Pentecost the religion of the monolithic God of Israel opened out into a new dimension with the mystery of the Trinity at its heart.

Christian prayer can be personal and private or public and universal for there is no set pattern for prayer. Every minute of every day of the year prayer is rising like incense up into the silence. Sometimes there seems to be no answer, but we go on praying for pray we must.

The fragments I have chosen to quote may not be amongst the loveliest or the best from the rich treasuries of Christian prayer, but for me they represent a few that I have strung through the thread of my life like beads upon a rosary.

KING ALFRED'S PRAYER

Guide me to Thy will to the need of my soul better than I can myself. Steadfast my mind towards Thy will and to my soul's need. Strengthen me against the temptations of the devil, and put far from me every unrighteousness. Shield me against my foes, seen and unseen; and teach me to do Thy will, that I may inwardly love Thee before all things with a clean mind and clean body. For Thou art my maker and my redeemer, my help, my comfort, my trust and my hope.

Amen.

THE DOOR OF THIS HOUSE

O God, make the door of this house wide enough to receive all who need human love and fellowship and narrow enough to shut out all envy, pride and strife. Make its threshold smooth enough to be no stumbling block, but rugged and strong enough to turn back the tempter's power. God make the door of this house the gateway to Thine everlasting kingdom, through Jesus Christ our Lord.

[Noted in the entrance hall of the Home of Divine Healing at Crowhurst in Sussex]

AT REST FROM OURSELVES

Lift up our souls to the pure bright serene light of Thy presence, that there we may breathe freely, there repose in Thy love, there be at rest from ourselves, and thence return, arrayed in Thy peace, to do and bear what shall please Thee.

[Pusey]

THE MEDICINE FOR ALL ILLS

O Lord God of Compassions, stretch out Thine hand and grant that all the sick may be healed. Grant them to be granted worthy of health. May His holy name be to them a medicine.

[Fourth century]

ALONE

Prayer is the burden of a sigh,
The falling of a tear—
The upward glancing of an eye
When none but God is near.

[Montgomery]

BATTER MY HEART

Batter my heart, three person'd God; for, you
As yet but knocke, breathe, shine, and seeke to mend;
That I may rise, and stand, o'erthrow mee and bend
Your force, to breake, blowe, burne and make me new.
I, like an usurpt towne, to another due.
Labour to admit you, but Oh, to no end,
Reason your viceroy in mee, mee should defend,
But is captiv'd, and proves weake or untrue.
Yey dearly I love you, and would be loved faine,
But am betroth'd unto your enemie:
Divorce mee, untie, or breake that knot againe,
Take mee to you, imprison mee, for I
Except you enthrall mee, never shall be free,
Nor ever chast, except you ravish me.

[Johne Donne (1572–1631; Doctor of Divinity, Cambridge and Dean of St Paul's)]

ONE THING MORE

Thou that hast given so much to me,
Give one thing more—a grateful heart.

[George Herbert, 1593–1632]

The following is a verse from my own favourite hymn, written by an American Quaker, the son of a farmer; a nature lover, a journalist and a poet. Although a hymn it has its place in my rosary of prayers, for what is this lovely hymn but a prayer set to music?

THE DEWS OF QUIETNESS

Drop Thy still dews of quietness
Till all our strivings cease,
Take from our lives the strain and stress
And let our ordered lives confess
The beauty of Thy peace.

[John Greenleaf Whittier, (1807–92)]

ASKING A BIG THING

Thou art coming to a King!
Large petitions with thee bring!
For His grace and power are such
None can ever ask too much.

[Newton]

TWO NIGHTS TO A DAY

Who goes to bed and does not pray,
Maketh two nights to every day.

[George Herbert]

Lord, teach us to pray.

[Luke, Chapter XI, verse 1]

NO POWER OF OURSELVES

Almighty God, who seest that we have no power of ourselves to help ourselves; Keep us both outwardly in our bodies and inwardly in our souls; that we may be defended from all adversities which may happen to the body, and from all evil thoughts which may assault and hurt the soul.

[Collect for the Second Sunday in Lent]

CRAMPED QUARTERS

Narrow is the mansion of my soul; enlarge Thou it, that Thou mayest enter in. It is ruinous; repair Thou it. It has that within which must offend Thine eyes; I confess and know it.

But who shall cleanse it? or to whom should I cry, save Thee? Lord, cleanse me from my secret faults, and spare Thy servant from the power of the enemy. I believe, and therefore do I speak. Lord, Thou knowest. Have I not confessed against myself my transgressions unto Thee, and Thou, my God, has forgiven the iniquity of my heart? I contend not in judgment with Thee, who art the truth; I fear to deceive myself; lest my iniquity lie unto itself. Therefore I contend not in judgment with Thee; for if Thou, Lord, shouldest mark iniquities, O Lord, who shall abide it?

[From The Confessions of St Augustine]

THE FEVER OF LIFE

O Lord, support us all the day long of this troublous life, until the shades lengthen and the evening comes, and the busy world is hushed, the fever of life is over and our work is done. Then, Lord, in Thy mercy grant us safe lodging, a holy rest, and peace at the last, through Jesus Christ our Lord. Amen.

THE PEACE WHICH THE WORLD CANNOT GIVE

O God, from whom all holy desires, all good counsels, and all just works do proceed; Give unto thy servants that peace which the world cannot give; that both our hearts may be set to obey thy commandments, and also that by thee we being defended from the fear of our enemies may pass our time in rest and quietness; though the merits of Jesus Christ our Saviour. Amen.

[The Second Collect at Evening Prayer]

LOSING MYSELF TO FIND MYSELF

By false self-love I lost myself; and by seeking Thee alone and purely loving Thee, I found both myself and Thee; and by this love have reduced myself more deeply to nothing. Because Thou, O most sweet Lord, doest deal with me above all that I deserve, and above all that I dare hope or ask for. Blessed be Thou, O my God, for though I am unworthy of all good, yet Thy generosity and infinite goodness never cease to do good even to those that are ungrateful, and that are turned away far from Thee. O convert us to Thee that we may be thankful, humble, and devout; for Thou art our salvation, our courage and strength.

[From *The Imitation of Christ*, by Thomas à Kempis (1379–1471)]

WALLED IN

O let Thine enemies know that thou hast received England . . . into Thine own protection. Set a wall about it, O Lord, and ever more mightily defend it. Let it be a comfort to the afflicted, a help to the oppressed, and a defence to Thy church and people persecuted abroad. . . . Direct and go before our armies both by sea and land. Bless them and prosper them, and grant unto them Thy honourable success and victory.

[Queen Elizabeth 1533–1603, written when news came that the Armada had sailed, and read twice a week in all churches throughout the country. The prayers were answered as were the prayers of those who prayed for the protection of 'this England' at the time of the Dunkirk evacuation when once again we were saved by the 'defensive moat' of the English Channel.]

IN TIMES OF RESTLESSNESS AND BOREDOM

Take from me, O God, all tediousness of spirit, all impatience and unquietness. Let me possess myself in patience.

[Jeremy Taylor (1613–67)]

In presuming to change the pronouns I have shifted the emphasis from 'us' to 'me' and found this little bead of prayer to be helpful, for much of the tediousness of the daily chores eats into the inner quietude of the spirit unless we learn how to possess our souls in patience.

THE DAY RETURNS

The day returns and brings us the petty round of irritating concerns and duties. Help us to play the man, help us to perform them with laughter and kind faces, let cheerfulness abound with industry. Give us to go blithely on our business all this day, bring us to our resting beds weary and content and undishonoured, and grant us in the end the gift of sleep.

[Robert Louis Stevenson (1850–94),
written at Vailima]

THE RIGHT BLESSING

O Lord our God, teach us, we beseech Thee, to ask Thee aright for the right blessing. Steer Thou the vessel of our life towards Thyself, Thou tranquil Haven of all storm-tossed souls. Show us the course wherein we should go. Renew a willing spirit in us. Let Thy spirit curb our wayward senses, and guide and enable us into that which is our true good, to keep Thy laws, and in all our works evermore to rejoice in Thy glorious and gladdening presence. For Thine is the glory and praise from all Thy saints for ever and ever.

[St Basil (329–79)]

THE ART OF PATIENCE

Lord, teach me the art of patience whilst I am well, and give me the use of it when I am sick. In that day either lighten my burden or strengthen my back. Make me, who so often in my health have discovered my weakness presuming on my own strength, to be strong in my sickness when I rely solely on Thy assistance.

[Thomas Fuller (1608–61)]

FOR SERVING MY COUNTRY FAITHFULLY

May the great God whom I worship grant to my country, and for the benefit of Europe in general, a great and glorious victory; and may no misconduct in anyone tarnish it; and may humanity after victory be the predominant feature in the British Fleet. For myself, individually, I commit my life to Him that made me, and may His blessing alight on my endeavours for serving my country faithfully. To Him I resign myself and the just cause which it is entrusted to me to defend. Amen.

[Lord Nelson, on the eve of the
Battle of Trafalgar, 1805]

O Lord, Thou knowest how busy I must be this day. If I forget Thee, do not Thou forget me.

[Sir Jacob Astley, on his knees before the Battle of Edgehill, 1642]

THE EVERLASTING PRESENCE

God be in my head,
  And in my understanding;
God be in my eyes,
  And in my looking;
God be in my mouth,
  And in my speaking;
God be in my heart,
  And in my thinking;
God be at my end,
  And at my departing.

[Old Sarum Primer, 1558]

MAKE ME AN INSTRUMENT

Lord, make me an instrument of thy peace!
Where there is hatred, let me sow love;
Where there is injury, let me sow pardon;
Where there is doubt, faith;
Where there is despair, hope;
Where there is darkness, light;
Where there is sadness, joy.

[St Francis of Assisi, c. 1182–1226]

UNBROKEN AND UNBREAKABLE

An anvil, Lord—let me be an anvil, smitten but standing firm.

[Polycarp's Prayer, offered while being burned at the stake, A.D. 155]

THE SACRED AND THE SECULAR

Almighty God, by whom alone kings reign and princes decree justice, and from whom alone cometh all counsel, wisdom and understanding,

We, Thine unworthy servants, here gathered together in Thy name, do most humbly beseech Thee to send down the heavenly wisdom from above, to direct and guide us in all our consultations:

And grant that, we having Thy fear always before our eyes, and laying aside all private interests, prejudices, and partial affections, the result of all our counsels may be the glory of Thy blessed name, the maintenance of true religion and justice, and the safety, honour, and happiness of the Queen, the public welfare, peace and tranquillity of the realm, and the uniting and knitting together of the hearts of all persons and estates within the same in true Christian love and charity towards one another, Through Jesus Christ, our Lord and Saviour.

[The Prayer of the House of Commons. Composed by Sir Christopher Yelverton, M.P. for Northampton and Speaker of the House at some time during the sixteenth century. This prayer is used at every sitting of the House]

THE LORD'S OWN PRAYER

Our Father, which art in Heaven, Hallowed be thy Name. Thy kingdom come. Thy will be done, in earth as it is in heaven. Give us this day our daily bread. And forgive us our trespasses, as we forgive them that trespass against us. And lead us not into temptation; but deliver us from evil. Amen.

Our Lord's is the perfect prayer for all men under all circumstances because it prefaces supplication with adoration. Its interpretation as given by Mary Baker Eddy and read Sunday by Sunday in every Christian Science Church throughout the world brings out the two-fold nature of man's relationship with his Maker as worshipper and suppliant. Adoration enlarges the mind, pushing back the horizons; against the background of the eternal human problems can be seen in their right perspective. The needs of the body are measured against the needs of the soul, and a right balance established.

Our Father which art in heaven,
  Our Father–Mother God, all-harmonious,
Hallowed be Thy name.
  Adorable One.
Thy Kingdom come.
  Thy kingdom is come; Thou art ever-present.
Thy will be done on earth, as it is in heaven.
  Enable us to know,—as in heaven, so on earth,—God is omnipotent, supreme.
Give us this day our daily bread;
  Give us grace for to-day; feed the famished affections;
And forgive us our debts, as we forgive our debtors.
  And love is reflected in love;
And lead us not into temptation, but deliver us from evil;
  And God leadeth us not into temptation, but delivereth us from sin, disease and death.
For Thine is the kingdom, and the power and the glory, forever.
  For God is infinite, all-power, all Life, Truth, Love, over all, and All.

A FISHERMAN'S PRAYER

God grant that I may live to fish
  Until my dying day,
And when it comes to my last cast
  I'll then most humbly pray,
When in the Lord's safe landing-net
  I'm peacefully asleep,
That in His mercy I'll be judged
  As good enough to keep.

[Author Unknown]

God bless me, I can pray no more tonight
[From 'Pippa Passes', by Robert Browning (1812–89)]

CHAPTER FIVE

Words in Amber

Fragments of insects and rotted flakes of cones or barks are often found in amber, for being resinous it is able to solidify around them and hold them imprisoned in a bubble of transparent gold. In the same way, words become caught in the imagination and held, while others are carried away like seeds on the wind. Why should this be? Why should something that somebody once said linger on in your thoughts, never to be forgotten, while other things of more importance are forgotten? It is useless to ask, for it is just one more of the questions that mere mortals are unable to answer.

When I was a child I was afraid of death for I was always aware of it as a brooding presence even in moments of the greatest delight. Paddling at the seaside, climbing a tree, seeing fairies at a pantomime or smelling a rose in the back garden, I was telling myself that I had only so many summers in which to smell and pick roses, so many autumns during which to watch the turning leaves, only so many winters for seeing sugary frost on the grass and shadows on a firelit wall, only so many springs for picking primroses and having a new hat for Easter. It was a terrifying thought, so much did I love the world, but from the day that I first heard those words from Sir Thomas Browne's 'Urn

Burial': 'Ready to be anything in the ecstasy of being ever' the fear went out of dying and death became as wonderful to contemplate as life itself. Those words were not only the cancelling out of fear; they were inspiration. Ready to be anything. That was it. No more would it matter when, where or how. The only reality was the ecstasy of 'being ever'.

Oh the magic of our beautiful and flexible English language! May the best of it remain as an everlasting treasury for the oncoming generations.

We all have our own personal treasury of remembered words: the day when somebody said 'I love you' or the echo of somebody's last words of goodbye. Though sometimes things seem to slip below the level of consciousness, such words are fixed in the golden amber of memory, for it often happens that the heart remembers what the mind forgets.

TOWARDS THE RISING OF THE SUN

Thus they discoursed together till late at night; and, after they had committed themselves to their Lord for protection they betook themselves to rest. The Pilgrim they laid in a large upper chamber, whose window opened towards the sun-rising: the name of the chamber was Peace, where he slept till break of day.

[From *The Pilgrim's Progress*, by John Bunyan (1628–88)]

THE VALLEYS OF HUMILITY

Humility is the great ornament and jewel of Christian religion, that whereby it is distinguished from all the wisdom of the world; it is not having been taught by the wise men of the Gentiles, but first put into a discipline, by our Lord Jesus Christ, who propounded himself imitable by his disciples so signally in nothing as in the twin-sisters of meekness and humility. Learn of me, for I am meek and humble, and ye shall find rest unto your souls. . . . Never be ashamed of thy birth, or thy parents, or thy trade, or thy present employment, for the meanness or poverty of any of them: and when there is an occasion to speak of them; such an occasion as would invite you to speak of anything that pleases you, omit it not; but speak as readily and indifferently of thy meanness as of thy greatness. Primislaus the first king of Bohemia kept his country shoes always by him, to remember from whence he was raised: and Agathocles by the furniture of his table confessed, that from a potter he was raised to be the king of Sicily.

[From *Holy Living and Dying*, by Jeremy Taylor (1613–67)]

There is a strange little link here with the poet Keats. As he lay dying in the small room at the foot of the Spanish Steps in Rome in 1821, he asked his good friend Joseph Severn to read to him from Jeremy Taylor's *Holy Living and Dying*. I like to think that Keats who admitted to no formal religious creed found in these daily readings not only a comfort but a hope.

CALLING US HOME

Deep within us all there is an amazing inner sanctuary of the soul, a holy place, a Divine Centre, a speaking Voice, to which we may continuously return. Eternity is at our hearts, pressing upon our time-torn lives, warming us with intimations of an astounding destiny, calling us home unto Itself.

[Thomas R. Kelly, Quaker (1893–1941)]

THEN THE LORD IS IN THE HOUSE

When thou turnest toward good,
Christ is walking in thy wood.
When thy heart says, 'Father, pardon!'
Then the Lord is in thy garden.
When stern Duty wakes to watch,
Then His hand is on the latch.

But when Hope thy song doth rouse
Then the Lord is in the house.
When to love is all thy wit
Christ doth at thy table sit.

[From 'Approaches', by George MacDonald (1824–1905)]

PROTECTION

At Tara today in this fateful hour
I place all heaven with its power,
and the sun with its brightness,
and the snow with its whiteness,
and fire with all the strength it hath,
and lightning with its rapid wrath,
and the winds with their swiftness along their path,
and the sea with its deepness,
and the rocks with their steepness,
and the earth with its starkness:
all these I place, by God's almighty help and grace
between myself and the powers of darkness.

[The Rune of St Patrick]

THE CREAM OF ALL MY HEART

Thou hast granted my request,
  Thou hast heard me:
Thou didst note my working breast,
  Thou hast spared me.
Wherefore with my utmost art
  I will sing Thee,
And the cream of all my heart
  I will bring Thee.
Seven whole days, not one in seven,
  I will praise Thee.
In my heart, though not in heaven,
  I can raise Thee.

[From George Herbert's Hymn,
'King of Glory, King of Peace']

When He giveth quietness, who then can make trouble?

[Job, Chapter 34, verse 29]

DEEPER CHORDS

The pianist, playing on a short keyboard and looking for E flat, found it wasn't there and said to himself, 'Oh, well, I'll play it an octave lower!'

How like our lives, when limited, restricted, and sometimes frustrated. . . . How like our vision, when we cannot see into the world of the spirit we long so much to enter. . . . How like the veiling of the future, completely hidden from us when we are faced with indecision and yet must plan ahead.

Yet we can play our music an octave lower always in the same key and as well as we know how; faithful in the little things. . . . Let us give thanks for the deep chords of the lower octave in our everyday life, for they have a resonant beauty, a deep tenderness, a gracious living of their own. Let us look for it when the higher octave does not seem to be there.

[From *The Science of Thought Review* Clare Cameron]

I SAW A STRANGER

I saw a stranger yestreen,
  I put food in the eating place,
  drink in the drinking place,
  music in the music place,
  and in the sacred name of the Triune,
He blessed myself and my house,
My cattle and my dear ones,
And the lark said in her song
Often, often, often, goes the Christ in the stranger's guise.

[A Celtic Rune of Hospitality]

It is loveliness I seek, not lovely things.

[From *The Divine Adventure*, by Fiona Macleod]

To give unto them beauty for ashes, the oil of joy for mourning, the garment of praise for the spirit of heaviness, that they might be called trees of righteousness, the planting of the Lord that he might be glorified.

[Isaiah, Chapter 61, verse 3]

How beautiful upon the mountains are the feet of him that bringeth good tidings, that publisheth peace . . .

[Isaiah, Chapter 52, verse 7]

THE HEART WARMING THAT CHANGED THE HEART OF ENGLAND

On Wednesday 24th May (1738), he awoke and opened his Bible at the text, 'Whereby are given unto us exceeding great and precious promises, that by these ye might be partakers of the divine nature'. That morning he went to St Paul's and in the evening, very unwillingly, to a society in Aldersgate Street, where someone read Luther's preface to the Epistle to the Romans. 'About a quarter before nine, while he was describing the change which God works in the heart through faith in Christ,' Wesley relates, 'I felt my heart strangely warmed. I felt I did trust in Christ, Christ alone, for salvation: and an assurance was given to me that He had taken away my sins, even mine, and saved me from the law of sin and death.'

[From *John Wesley—Anglican*, by Garth Lean]

THE DAILY RESURRECTION

Receive, therefore, every day as a resurrection from death, as a new enjoyment of life; meet every rising sun with such sentiments of God's goodness, as if you had seen it, and all things, new created upon your account: and under the sense of so great a blessing, let your joyful heart praise and magnify so good and glorious a Creator.

[William Law (1686–1761)]

THE SHOEMAKER WHO KNEW IT ALL

Search where we will through the whole range of mysticism, it is hard to find a deeper or more interior mystic than the poor, unlettered shoemaker of Goerlitz, Jacob Boehme. Unlearned, as this world understands learning, he yet penetrated to the core of things, touching depths that the profoundest philosophers and the keenest thinkers have essayed in vain to reach. Where the most subtle metaphysicians have failed in their search for truth, this poor shoemaker, through his humble childlike faith, succeeded in discovering the ground of all things. Not only was he a great mystic, but he was also a spiritual occulist. . . . His wonderful humble-mindedness, his childlike attitude of mind, was the root cause of his profound knowledge. . . . When St Augustine was asked which was the first great Christian virtue he replied, 'Humility'. When asked which was the second he replied, 'Humility'; and which the third, he again replied 'Humility'. Humility is the foundation virtue, because it is the antithesis of pride, which is the root cause of all evil.

[From *Jacob Boehme*, 1574–1624, Chapters 1 and 12, by W. P. Swainson]

I am but a little child: I know not how to go out or come in.

[Spoken by King Solomon, the wisest man of his generation—I Kings, Chapter 3, verse 7]

THE MAKER, THE LOVER, THE KEEPER

In this He showed me a little thing, the quantity of a hazel nut, lying in the palm of my hand, and to my understanding it was as round as any ball. I looked thereupon and thought: 'What may this be'? And I was answered in a general way, thus: 'It is all that is made'. I marvelled how it could last, for methought it might fall suddenly to naught for littleness. And I was answered in my understanding: 'It lasts and ever shall last because God loves it, and so hath all-thing its being through the love of God.'

In this little thing I saw three parts. The first is that God made it; the second is that He loves it; the third is that God keeps it. But what is that to me? In sooth, the Maker, the Lover, the Keeper.

[Julian of Norwich, the fourteenth-century visionary]

FIRE IN THE DARK

By the expression 'burning' we understand some of the sweet effects which are wrought in the soul by the dark night of contemplation: for occasionally, amid the darkness, the soul receives light—'light shineth in darkness—' the mystical inflowing streaming directly into the understanding, while the will remains dry, that is, not reaching to actual union, but with a calmness and pureness so exquisite and so delicious to the soul as to be utterly indescribable.

[From *The Dark Night Of The Soul*, by St John of the Cross, Spanish mystic (sixteenth century)]

CAUSE AND EFFECT

The Lord of all, himself through all diffused,
Sustains, and is the life of all that lives.
  Nature is but a name for an effect,
Whose cause is God.

[From 'The Task', by William Cowper (1731–1800)]

CONTINUALLY TO HAPPINESS

They who are in the stream of Providence are borne continually to happiness, whatever may be the appearance of the means. They are in the stream of Providence who put their trust in the Divine and attribute all things to Him; and they are not in the stream of Providence who trust in themselves alone.

All things succeed for a happy state to eternity with those who put their trust in the Divine, and all that befalls them in time is then conducive to this end. So far as anyone is in the stream of Providence, he is in a state of peace.

[From *Heavenly Arcana*, by Swedenborg, scientist, mystic and philosopher (born in Stockholm 1688, died in London 1772)]

CRISIS WITHIN THE DIVINE ENVIRONMENT

What is happening under our eyes within the mass of people? What is the cause of this disorder in society? this uneasy agitation, these swelling waves, these whirling and mingling currents and these turbulent and formidable new impulses? Mankind is visibly passing through a crisis of growth. Mankind is becoming dimly aware of its shortcomings and its capacities. And as we said on the first page it sees the universe growing luminous like the horizon just before sunrise. It has a sense of premonition and of expectation. . . . All over the world, men are toiling in laboratories, in studios, in deserts, in factories, in the vast social crucible. The ferment that is taking place by their instrumentality in art and science and thought is happening for your sake. Open then, your arms and your heart, like Christ your Lord, and welcome the waters, the flood and the sap of humanity. Accept it, this sap—for, without its baptism, you will wither, without desire, like a flower out of water; and tend it, since, without your sun, it will disperse itself wildly in sterile shoots.

The temptations of too large a world, the seductions of too beautiful a world—where are these now?

They do not exist.

Now the earth can certainly clasp me in her giant arms. She can swell me with her life, or take me back into her dust. She can deck herself out for me with every charm, with every horror, with every mystery. She can intoxicate me with her perfume of tangibility and unity. She can cast me to my knees in expectation of what is maturing in her breast . . .

But her enchantments can no longer do me harm, since she has become for me, over and above herself, the body of Him who is and of Him who is coming. The divine milieu.

[From *Le Milieu Divin*, by Pierre Teilhard de Chardin (written in Tientsin in 1926–7)]

READY TO BE ANYTHING

Lastly; if length of days be thy portion, make it not thy expectation. Reckon not upon long life: think every day the last, and live always beyond thy account. . . . Time past is gone like a shadow; make time to come present. . . . Ready to be anything, in the ecstasy of being ever.

[From Sir Thomas Browne's 'Religio Medici' (1605–82)]

NOTHING HAPPENS BY CHANCE

Nothing that happens in the world happens by chance. God is a God of order. Everything is arranged upon definite principles, and never at random. The world, even the religious world, is governed by law. Character is governed by law. Happiness is governed by law. The Christian experiences are governed by law. Men, forgetting this, expect Rest, Joy, Peace, Faith, to drop into their souls from the air like snow or rain. But in point of fact they do not do so; and if they did they would no less have their origin in previous activities and be controlled by natural laws. Rain and snow do drop from the air, but not without a long previous history. They are the mature effects of former causes. Equally so are Rest, and Peace, and Joy. They too, have each a previous history. Storms and winds and calms are not accidents, but are brought about by antecedent circumstances. Rest and Peace are but calms in man's inward nature, and arise through causes as definite and as inevitable. Realise it thoroughly: it is a methodical not an accidental world.

[From *The Greatest Thing In The World*, Chapter V, by Henry Drummond (1851–97)]

THE LAMP THAT LIT ALL EUROPE

Let us approach that sacred isle with more than common reverence: there, where now it lies in the midst of rolling billows, and listening but to sea-birds' cries, from age to age in the morning of early history, night and day it heard the sweet songs of God.

[Bishop Ewing. From *An Iona Anthology*. Edited by F. Marian McNeill]

In the little island of Iona a lamp was lit whose flame lighted pagan Europe, and what a holy and beautiful place it is! Columba pronounced a benediction upon it when, having come from Ireland, those in the little coracle first sighted its shores.

Behold Iona!
A blessing on each eye that seeth it!
He who does a good for others
Here will find his own redoubled
Many-fold!

[Attributed to Columba]

It is of interest to note that St Columba founded the first Iona Community before Augustine came to Canterbury to convert the British, sent by Pope Gregory. He must have been surprised to have found that there was already a Christian church established there, and that the wife of the King of Kent was a Christian. I wonder how soon he discovered what was going on in Glastonbury and Iona. The second Iona Community has now been established under the inspiration of the Revd George Macleod and the Abbey restored to its former glory.

A MAN OF ONE BOOK

To candid, reasonable men, I am not afraid to lay open what have been the inmost thoughts of my heart. I have thought, I am a creature of a day, passing through life as an arrow through the air. I am a spirit come from God, and returning to God; just hovering over the great gulf; till, a few moments hence, I am no more seen; I drop into an unchangeable eternity! I want to know one thing,—the way to heaven; how to land safe on that happy shore. God Himself has condescended to teach the way: for this very end He came from heaven. He hath written it down in a book. O give me that book! At any price, give me the book of God! I have it. Here is knowledge enough for me. Let me be homo unius libri.

[From 'Preface to Sermons', *Works*, Vol. 2, by John Wesley (1703–91)]

TOO MUCH OF EVERYTHING

In the overabundance of certain things I find vulgarity. Thus I object to an overcrowding of furniture in the sitting room, to a whole bunch of writing brushes beside the ink-slab, too many images of the Buddha in the chapel, too great a profusion of stones, trees and grass in a garden, too many children in a house, too many words to a friend, too verbose dedications of sacred offerings. Things that I feel can never be overdone are books in the book receptacles and rubbish on the rubbish heap!

[Kenko]

How right he was, that thirteenth-century hermit-monk writing in his solitary hut in the Hills of Storm! It has been said that few writers had a better understanding than Kenko of what the Japanese call, 'the Ah-ness of things'.

BURY ME IF YOU CAN CATCH ME

Before drinking the fatal cup of hemlock Socrates was asked 'How would you be buried?' to which he replied, 'Just as you please, if you can but catch me, and I not elude your pursuit'.

FIDDLESTICKS

If it was difficult for Margaret to understand; it was even more so for his wife, that good woman of direct speech and common sense. Having obtained permission to visit him (imprisoned in the Tower of London), she came quickly to her opinion: 'What, the good year, Master More, I marvel at you, that have been always hitherto taken for so wise a man, will now so play the fool to lie here in this close, filthy prison, and be content thus to be shut up thus among mice and rats, when you might be abroad at your liberty, and with the favour and goodwill both of the King and his Council, if you would but do as all the Bishops and the best learned of this realm have done; and seeing you have at Chelsea a right fair house, your library, your books, your gallery, your garden, your orchard, and all other necessaries so handsome about you, where you might, in the company of me, your wife, your children and household, be merry, I muse what a gods name you mean here still thus fondly to tarry.

More gave his answer with a smile: 'I pray thee, good Mistress Alice, tell me one thing.'

'What is it?'

'Is not this house as near heaven as my own?'

'Tillie valle, Tillie valle!' was her impatient reply.

[From *The Story of Thomas More*, Chapter 16, by John Farrow]

This, I presume, meant something like 'fiddlesticks' or 'nonsense' with which she dismissed in exasperation Sir Thomas's rich blending of wit and piety.

EVERY DAY'S MOST QUIET NEED

How do I love thee? Let me count the ways,
I love thee to the depth and breadth and height
My soul can reach, when feeling out of sight
For the ends of Being and ideal Grace.
I love thee to the level of every day's
Most quiet need, by sun and candlelight.

[From a poem by Elizabeth Barrett Browning (1806–61)]

CHAPTER SIX

Precious Stones of Scripture

The precious stones of holy scripture form the foundation stones of western civilisation. Many ecclesiastical structures of dogma have been raised upon these stones. Naturally so, for although communist doctrine asserts that all men are equal, it is the opposite of what is true: every man is different and within the framework of the Christian religion there is accommodation for the simple and the wise, the saint and the sinner, the white man and the black. Equality means uniformity and uniformity is death to the religious spirit.

In spite of unceasing efforts to undermine and discredit the Bible, it remains unassailable.

The Bible is the authentic record of the history of the Israel peoples, created by God through the miracle birth of Isaac and through whom He was to work out the salvation of the human race from the calling of Abraham to the revelations on Patmos. Here in the Bible is the first chronicled appearance of man on this earth. We need go no further back than 4004 B.C. Whether we wriggled out of the slime of the seabed or sprang from apes like rabbits out of a conjurer's hat need not concern us. The theory of blind automatic evolution is far more fantastic than anything in Genesis, so it is reasonable to say that the proper study of man comes within the compass of the Bible.

The humanists are out to have religious education abolished from school curricula. Why, I wonder, are they so afraid of the Bible? No matter how many academic qualifications a student may possess, if he is Biblically illiterate he can never consider himself to be educated. Not only does he suffer an intellectual and cultural deprivation if launched on the world with no knowledge of the greatest book in the world, but he is deprived of something even more precious: a foundation stone on which to build his life.

Economy of space has compelled me to omit lines in some of the more lengthy psalms, but not a word can be spared from the 55th chapter of Isaiah. Shall I ever forget the impact that it made on my mind when I was made to learn it by heart at the age of six?

FREE FOR ALL

Ho, every one that thirsteth, come ye to the waters and he that hath no money; come ye, buy, and eat; yea, come, buy wine and milk without money and without price.
Wherefore do ye spend money for that which is not bread? and your labour for that which satisfieth not? hearken diligently unto me, and eat ye that which is good, and let your soul delight itself in fatness.
Incline your ear, and come unto me: hear, and your soul shall live; and I will make an everlasting covenant with you, even the sure mercies of David.
Behold, I have given him for a witness to the people, a leader and commander to the people.
Behold, thou shalt call a nation that thou knowest not, and nations that knew not thee shall run unto thee because of the Lord thy God, and for the Holy One of Israel; for he hath glorified thee.
Seek ye the Lord while he may be found, call ye upon him while he is near:
Let the wicked forsake his way, and the unrighteous man his thoughts: and let him return unto the Lord, and he will have mercy upon him; and to our God, for he will abundantly pardon.
For my thoughts are not your thoughts, neither are your ways my ways, saith the Lord.
For as the heavens are higher than the earth, so are my ways higher than your ways, and my thoughts than your thoughts.
For as the rain cometh down, and the snow from heaven, and returneth not thither, but watereth the earth, and maketh it bring forth and bud, that it may give seed to the sower, and bread to the eater:
So shall my word be that goeth forth out of my mouth: it shall not return unto me void but it shall accomplish that which I please, and it shall prosper in the thing whereto I sent it.
For ye shall go out with joy, and be led forth with peace: the mountains and the hills shall break forth before you into singing, and all the trees of the field shall clap their hands.
Instead of the thorn shall come up the fir tree, and instead of

the brier shall come up the myrtle tree: and it shall be to the Lord for a name, for an everlasting sign that shall not be cut off.

[Isaiah, Chapter 55]

HATH GOD FORGOTTEN TO BE GRACIOUS?

I cried unto God with my voice, even unto God with my voice; and he gave ear unto me.

In the day of my trouble I sought the Lord: my sore ran in the night, and ceased not: my soul refused to be comforted.

I remembered God and was troubled: I complained and my spirit was overwhelmed.

Thou holdest mine eyes waking: I am so troubled that I cannot speak.

I have considered the days of old, the years of ancient times.

I call to remembrance my song in the night: I commune with mine own heart: and my spirit made diligent search.

Will the Lord cast off for ever? and will he be favourable no more?

Is his mercy clean gone for ever? doth his promise fail for evermore?

Hath God forgotten to be gracious? hath he in anger shut up his tender mercies?

And I said, This is my infirmity: but I will remember the years of the right hand of the most High.

I will remember the works of the Lord: surely I will remember the wonders of old.

I will meditate also of all thy work, and talk of thy doings.

Thy way, O God, is in the sanctuary: who is so great a God as our God?

Thou art the God that doest wonders: thou has declared thy strength among the people.

Thou hast with thine arm redeemed thy people, the sons of Jacob and Joseph.

The waters saw thee, O God, the waters saw thee; they were afraid: the depths also were troubled.

The clouds poured out water: the skies sent out a sound: thine arrows also went abroad.

The voice of thy thunder was in the heaven: the lightnings lightened the world: the earth trembled and shook.
Thy way is in the sea, and thy path in the great waters, and thy footsteps are not known.
Thou leddest thy people like a flock by the hand of Moses and Aaron.

[Psalm 77]

A LAMP UNTO MY FEET

Thy word is a lamp unto my feet and a light unto my path.
I have sworn, and I will perform it, that I will keep thy righteous judgments.
I am afflicted very much: quicken me, O Lord, according to thy word.
Accept, I beseech thee, the freewill offerings of my mouth, O Lord, and teach me thy judgments.
My soul is continually in my hand, yet I do not forget thy law.
The wicked have laid a snare for me: yet I erred not from thy precepts.
Thy testimonies have I taken as an heritage for ever: for they are the rejoicing of my heart.
I have inclined mine heart to perform thy statutes alway, even unto the end.

[From Psalm 119, verses 105–112]

A little over a thousand years later Our Lord, whose coming was heralded by the light of a star said 'Ye are the light of the world. A city that is set on a hill cannot be hid, Neither do men light a candle, and put it under a bushel, but on a candlestick; and it giveth light to all that are in the house. Let your light so shine before men, that they may see your good works, and glorify your Father which is in heaven'.

We cannot be a light either in the house or in the world unless our path be illuminated by the lamp of the Word of God.

THE SECRET PLACE

He that dwelleth in the secret place of the most High shall abide under the shadow of the Almighty
I will say of the Lord, He is my refuge and my fortress: my God; in him will I trust.
Surely he shall deliver thee from the snare of the fowler, and from the noisome pestilence.
He shall cover thee with his feathers, and under his wings shalt thou trust: his truth shall be thy shield and buckler.
Thou shalt not be afraid for the terror by night; nor for the arrow that flieth by day;
Nor for the pestilence that walketh in darkness; nor for the destruction that wasteth at noonday.
A thousand shall fall at thy side, and ten thousand at thy right hand; but it shall not come nigh thee.
Only with thine eyes shalt thou behold and see the reward of the wicked.
Because thou has made the Lord, which is my refuge, even the most High, thy habitation;
There shall no evil befall thee, neither shall any plague come nigh thy dwelling.
For he shall give his angels charge over thee, to keep thee in all thy ways.
They shall bear thee up in their hands, lest thou dash thy foot against a stone.
Thou shalt tread upon the lion and adder: the young lion and the dragon shalt thou trample under feet.
Because he hath set his love upon me, therefore will I deliver him: I will set him on high, because he hath known my name.
He shall call upon me, and I will answer him: I will be with him in trouble; I will deliver him and honour him.
With long life will I satisfy him, and shew him my salvation.

[Psalm 91]

WHO HEALETH ALL THY DISEASES

Bless the Lord, O my soul: and all that is within me, bless his holy name.

Bless the Lord, O my soul, and forget not all his benefits:
Who forgiveth all thine iniquities; who healeth all thy diseases;
Who redeemeth thy life from destruction; who crowneth thee with lovingkindness and tender mercies;
Who satisfieth thy mouth with good things; so that thy youth is renewed like the eagle's.
The Lord executeth righteousness and judgment for all that are oppressed.
He made known his ways unto Moses, his acts unto the children of Israel.
The Lord is merciful and gracious, slow to anger, and plenteous in mercy.
He will not always chide: neither will he keep his anger for ever.
He hath not dealt with us after our sins; nor rewarded us according to our iniquities.
For as the heaven is high above the earth, so great is his mercy toward them that fear him.
As far as the east is from the west, so far hath he removed our transgressions from us.
Like as a father pitieth his children, so the Lord pitieth them that fear him.
For he knoweth our frame; he remembereth that we are dust.
As for man, his days are as grass: as a flower of the field, so he flourisheth.
For the wind passeth over it, and it is gone; and the place thereof shall know it no more.
But the mercy of the Lord is from everlasting to everlasting upon them that fear him, and his righteousness unto children's children;
To such as keep his covenant and to those that remember his commandments to do them.
The Lord hath prepared his throne in the heavens; and his kingdom ruleth over all.
Bless the Lord, ye his angels, that excel in strength, that do his commandments, hearkening unto the voice of his word.
Bless ye the Lord, all ye his hosts; ye ministers of his that do his pleasure.

Bless the Lord, all his works in all places of his dominion: bless the Lord, O my soul.

[Psalm 103]

I WILL SUP WITH HIM

Behold, I stand at the door and knock: if any man hear my voice, and open the door, I will come in to him, and will sup with him, and he with me.

[Revelation, Chapter 3, verse 20]

THE INCARNATION OF GOD

And the Word was made flesh, and dwelt among us, (and we beheld his glory, the glory as of the only begotten of the Father) full of grace and truth.

[John, Chapter 1, verse 14]

A LIVING SACRIFICE

I beseech you therefore brethren, by the mercies of God, that you present your bodies a living sacrifice, holy, acceptable unto God, which is your reasonable service. And be not conformed to this world; but be ye transformed by the renewing of your mind. . . .

[Romans, Chapter 12, verses 1–2]

THE EARTH IS FULL OF THY RICHES

Bless the Lord, O my soul. O Lord my God, thou art very great; thou art clothed with honour and majesty.
Who coverest thyself with light as with a garment: who stretchest out the heavens like a curtain:
Who layeth the beams of his chambers in the waters: who maketh the clouds his chariot: who walketh upon the wings of the wind:
Who maketh his angels spirits; his ministers a flaming fire:

Who laid the foundations of the earth, that it should not be removed for ever.
Thou coveredst it with the deep as with a garment: the waters stood above the mountains.
At thy rebuke they fled; at the voice of thy thunder they hasted away.
They go up by the mountains; they go down by the valleys unto the place which thou has founded for them.
Thou hast set a bound that they may not pass over; that they turn not again to cover the earth.
He sendeth the springs into the valleys, which run among the hills.
They give drink to every beast of the field: the wild asses quench their thirst.
By them shall the fowls of the heaven have their habitation, which sing among the branches.
He watereth the hills from his chambers: the earth is satisfied with the fruit of thy works.
He causeth the grass to grow for the cattle, and herb for the service of man: that he may bring forth food out of the earth;
And wine that maketh glad the heart of man, and oil to make his face to shine, and bread which strengtheneth man's heart.
The trees of the Lord are full of sap; the cedars of Lebanon which he hath planted;
Where the birds make their nests: as for the stork the fir trees are her house.
The high hills are a refuge for the wild goats; and the rocks for the conies.
He appointed the moon for seasons: the sun knoweth his going down.
Thou makest darkness, and it is night: wherein all the beasts of the forest do creep forth.
The young lions roar after their prey, and seek their meat from God.
The sun ariseth, they gather themselves together and lay them down in their dens.
Man goeth forth unto his work and to his labour until the evening

O Lord, how manifold are thy works! in wisdom hast thou made them all: the earth is full of thy riches.
So is the great and wide sea, wherein are things creeping innumerable, both small and great beasts.
There go the ships: there is that leviathan, whom thou hast made to play therein.
These wait all upon thee; that thou mayest give them their meat in due season.
That thou givest them they gather: thou openest thine hand, they are filled with good.
Thou hidest thy face, they are troubled: thou takest away their breath, they die and return to their dust.
Thou sendest forth thy spirit, they are created: and thou renewest the face of the earth.
The glory of the Lord shall endure for ever: the Lord shall rejoice in his works.
He looketh on the earth, and it trembleth: he toucheth the hills and they smoke.
I will sing unto the Lord as long as I live: I will sing praise to my God while I have my being.
My meditation of him shall be sweet: I will be glad in the Lord.
Let the sinners be consumed out of the earth, and let the wicked be no more. Bless thou the Lord, O my soul. Praise ye the Lord.

[Psalm 104]

This lovely psalm might be called a hymn in praise of creation. It is a reminder that everything required for the sustenance and the delight of man comes out of the earth or the sea: flowers, fruit, gold, corn, oil, wine, fish. And the beasts fatten on the grass that clothes this marvellous thing we call 'earth', giving us meat, milk, horn and hides. It is indeed a wonderful world. But what have we made of it? It should be remembered that the water we pollute and the soil we misuse is not ours to destroy. We are but trustees, for the earth and its riches belong to Him who made it.

SWEETER THAN HONEY

O how I love thy law! It is my meditation all the day.
Thou through thy commandments hast made me wiser than mine enemies: for they are ever with me.
I have more understanding than all my teachers: for thy testimonies are my meditation.
I understand more than the ancients, because I keep thy precepts.
I have refrained my feet from every evil way, that I might keep thy word.
I have not departed from thy judgments: for thou hast taught me.
How sweet are thy words unto my taste! yea, sweeter than honey to my mouth!
Through thy precepts I get understanding: therefore I hate every false way.

[From Psalm 119, verses 97–104]

GREEN PASTURES

The Lord is my shepherd; I shall not want. He maketh me to lie down in green pastures: he leadeth me beside the still waters.
He restoreth my soul: he leadeth me in the paths of righteousness for his name's sake.
Yea, though I walk through the valley of the shadow of death, I will fear no evil: for thou art with me; thy rod and thy staff they comfort me.
Thou preparest a table before me in the presence of mine enemies: thou anointest my head with oil; my cup runneth over.
Surely goodness and mercy shall follow me all the days of my life: and I will dwell in the house of the Lord for ever.

[Psalm 23]

There is a story told of an actor on holiday from London who thought that he could give a better rendering of the 23rd Psalm than the vicar of the local church and suggested that he be allowed to read it from the pulpit on the following

Sunday. The vicar with his homely north country accent read the psalm in his usual manner with no attempt at making an impression. Next came the actor whose rich cultivated voice filled the old church with its beauty, every lovely sentence receiving its full measure of expression by the art of a professional. But something in the silence and in his own heart told him that his performance had been a flop. 'Splendid' said the vicar later as the two men shook hands in the porch. 'No', said the actor 'I know the psalm. You know the Shepherd.'

OF THE EARTH EARTHY

In the beginning God created the heaven and the earth.
And the earth was without form, and void; and darkness was upon the face of the deep. And the spirit of God moved upon the face of the waters.
And God said, Let there be light: and there was light.
And God saw the light, that it was good: and God divided the light from the darkness.
And God called the light Day, and the darkness he called Night. And the evening and the morning were the first day.
And God said, Let there be a firmament in the midst of the waters, and let it divide the waters from the waters.
And God made the firmament, and divided the waters which were under the firmament from the waters which were above the firmament: and it was so.
And God called the firmament Heaven. And the evening and the morning were the second day.
And God said, Let the waters under the heaven be gathered together unto one place, and let the dry land appear: and it was so.
And God called the dry land Earth; and the gathering together of the waters called he Seas: and God saw that it was good.
And God said, Let the earth bring forth grass, the herb yielding seed, and the fruit tree yielding fruit after his kind, whose seed is in itself, upon the earth: and it was so.
And the earth brought forth grass, and herb yielding seed after

his kind, and the tree yielding fruit, whose seed was in itself, after his kind: and God saw that it was good.
And the evening and the morning were the third day.
And God said, Let there be lights in the firmament of the heaven to divide the day from the night; and let them be for signs, and for seasons, and for days and years:
And let them be for lights in the firmament of the heaven to give light upon the earth: and it was so.
And God made two great lights; the greater light to rule the day, and thc lesser light to rule the night: he made the stars also.
And God set them in the firmament of the heaven to give light upon the earth.
And to rule over the day and over the night, and to divide the light from the darkness: and God saw that it was good.
And the evening and the morning were the fourth day.
And God said, Let the waters bring forth abundantly the moving creature that hath life, and fowl that may fly above the earth in the open firmament of heaven.
And God created great whales, and every living creature that moveth, which the waters brought forth abundantly, after their kind, and every winged fowl after his kind: and God saw that it was good.
And God blessed them, saying, Be fruitful, and multiply, and fill the waters in the seas, and let fowl multiply in the earth.
And the evening and the morning were the fifth day.
And God said, Let the earth bring forth the living creature after his kind, cattle, and creeping thing, and beast of the earth after his kind: amd it was so.
And God made the beast of the earth after his kind, and cattle after their kind, and every thing that creepeth upon the earth after his kind: and God saw that it was good.
And God said, Let us make man in our image, after our likeness: and let them have dominion over the fish of the sea, and over the fowl of the air, and over the cattle, and over all the earth, and over every creeping thing that creepeth upon the earth.
So God created man in his own image, in the image of God

created he him; male and female created he them.

[Genesis, Chapter 1, verses 1–27]

AND MAN BECAME A LIVING SOUL

The timeless evolutionary processes that went into the making of man of the earth earthy came to their fulfilment in the creation of Adam, but man, in the following chapter, in being breathed upon by God evolves into a new dimension, and so we have the story of the second creation.

And the Lord God formed man of the dust of the ground, and breathed into his nostrils the breath of life; and man became a living soul.

[Genesis, Chapter 2, verse 7]

THE PROMISES

And the angel of the Lord called unto him out of heaven, and said, Abraham, Abraham: and he said, Here am I.

And he said, Lay not thine hand upon the lad, neither do thou any thing unto him; for now I know that thou fearest God, seeing thou has not withheld thy son, thine only son from me.

And Abraham lifted up his eyes, and looked, and behold behind him a ram caught in a thicket by his horns: and Abraham went and took the ram, and offered him up for a burnt offering in the stead of his son.

And Abraham called the name of that place Jehovah-jireh: as it is said to this day, In the mount of the Lord it shall be seen.

And the angel of the Lord called unto Abraham out of heaven the second time,

And said, By myself have I sworn, saith the Lord, for because thou hast done this thing, and hast not withheld thy son, thine only son:

That in blessing I will bless thee, and in multiplying I will multiply thy seed as the stars of the heaven, and as the sand which is upon the sea shore; and thy seed shall possess the gate of his enemies;

And in thy seed shall all the nations of the earth be blessed; because thou hast obeyed my voice.

[Genesis, Chapter 22, verses 11–18]

As a reward for his unquestioning obedience God promised Abraham that through his descendants all the nations of the earth would be blessed. Was that promise fulfilled? Obviously not in the tribe of Judah. Judah had the honour of bringing forth the Messiah and the dishonour of crucifying him. It is in the history of the ten lost tribes of Israel, as distinct from Judah, that we must look for the interpretation and fulfilment of the promise.

TOUCH ALL THAT HE HATH AND HE WILL CURSE THEE

Now there was a day when the sons of God came to present themselves before the Lord, and Satan came also among them. And the Lord said unto Satan, Whence comest thou? Then Satan answered the Lord, and said, From going to and fro in the earth, and from walking up and down in it.

And the Lord said unto Satan, Hast thou considered my servant Job, that there is none like him in the earth, a perfect and an upright man, one that feareth God and escheweth evil?

Then Satan answered the Lord, and said, Doth Job fear God for nought?

Hast not thou made an hedge about him, and about his house, and about all that he hath on every side? thou hast blessed the work of his hands, and his substance is increased in the land.

But put forth thine hand now, and touch all that he hath, and he will curse thee to thy face.

[Job, Chapter 1, verses 6–11]

God allowed Satan to bring a series of catastrophes upon the blameless Job in order to prove that he could take it and not lose his faith. He did and he could. But Mrs Job had no patience with such stubbornness. 'Dost thou still retain thine integrity?' she railed. 'Curse God, and die.' But Job was not to be tempted into the slush of self-pity and herein lies a lesson for us all. 'Thou speaketh as one of the foolish women speaketh', he replied. 'What! Shall we receive good at the hand of God, and shall we not receive evil?' It is good to read in the final chapter that the faithfulness of Job did not go unrewarded.

> And the Lord turned the captivity of Job, when he prayed for his friends: also the Lord gave Job twice as much as he had before.
>
> [Job, Chapter 42, verse 10]

INTREAT ME NOT TO LEAVE THEE

. . . and Orpah kissed her mother in law; but Ruth clave unto her.
And she said, Behold, thy sister in law is gone back unto her people, and unto her gods: return thou after thy sister in law.
And Ruth said, Intreat me not to leave thee, or to return from following after thee: for whither thou goest, I will go, and where thou lodgest, I will lodge: thy people shall be my people, and thy God my God:
Where thou diest, will I die, and there will I be buried: the Lord do so to me, and more also, if ought but death part thee and me.

When she saw that she was stedfastly minded to go with her, then she left speaking unto her.
So they two went until they came to Bethlehem. And it came to pass, when they were come to Bethlehem, that all the city was moved about them, and they said, Is this Naomi?
And she said unto them, Call me not Naomi, call me Mara: for the Almighty hath dealt very bitterly with me.
I went out full, and the Lord hath brought me home again empty: why then call ye me Naomi, seeing the Lord hath testified against me, and the Almighty hath afflicted me?
So Naomi returned, and Ruth the Moabitess, her daughter in law, with her, which returned out of the country of Moab:

and they came to Bethlehem in the beginning of the barley harvest.

[Ruth, Chapter 1, verses 14–22]

Did any young widow ever speak lovelier words to her mother-in-law than were spoken by Ruth to Naomi? It is interesting to note that her faithfulness gave her a place in history, for later she married Boaz and their son was named Obed who became the grandfather of David from whose line our Lord Himself was descended.

CHARITY

Though I speak with the tongues of men and of angels, and have not charity, I am become as sounding brass, or a tinkling cymbal.

And though I have the gift of prophecy, and understand all mysteries, and all knowledge; and though I have all faith, so that I could remove mountains, and have not charity, I am nothing.

And though I bestow all my goods to feed the poor, and though I give my body to be burned, and have not charity, it profiteth me nothing.

Charity suffereth long, and is kind; charity envieth not; charity vaunteth not itself, is not puffed up.

Doth not behave itself unseemly, seeketh not her own, is not easily provoked, thinketh no evil;

Rejoiceth not in iniquity, but rejoiceth in the truth;

Beareth all things, believeth all things, hopeth all things, endureth all things.

Charity never faileth: but whether there be prophecies, they shall fail; whether there be tongues, they shall cease; whether there be knowledge, it shall vanish away.

For we know in part, and we prophesy in part.

But when that which is perfect is come, then that which is in part shall be done away.

When I was a child, I spake as a child, I understood as a child: but when I became a man, I put away childish things.

For now we see through a glass darkly; but then face to face;

now I know in part; but then shall I know even as also I am known.
And now abideth faith, hope, charity. these three; but the greatest of these is charity.

[1 Corinthians, Chapter 13]

AND THE SPIRIT SHALL RETURN

Remember now thy Creator in the days of thy youth, while the evil days come not, nor the years draw nigh, when thou shalt say, I have no pleasure in them;
While the sun, or the light, or the moon, or the stars, be not darkened, nor the clouds return after the rain:
In the day when the keepers of the house shall tremble, and the strong men shall bow themselves, and the grinders cease because they are few, and those that look out of the windows be darkened,
And the doors shall be shut in the streets, when the sound of the grinding is low, and he shall rise up at the voice of the bird, and all the daughters of music shall be brought low;
Also when they shall be afraid of that which is high, and fears shall be in the way, and the almond tree shall flourish, and the grasshopper shall be a burden, and desire shall fail: because man goeth to his long home, and the mourners go about the streets:
Or ever the silver cord be loosed, or the golden bowl be broken, or the pitcher be broken at the fountain, or the wheel broken at the cistern.
Then shall the dust return to the earth as it was: and the spirit shall return unto God who gave it.

[Ecclesiastes, Chapter 12, verses 1–7]

HAPPY ARE THEY

Blessed are the poor in spirit: for theirs is the kingdom of heaven.
Blessed are they that mourn; for they shall be comforted.
Blessed are the meek; for they shall inherit the earth.
Blessed are they which do hunger and thirst after righteousness: for they shall be filled.

Blessed are the merciful: for they shall obtain mercy.
Blessed are the pure in heart: for they shall see God.
Blessed are the peacemakers: for they shall be called the children of God.

[Matthew, Chapter 5, verses 3–9
(The Sermon on the Mountain)]

ALL THINGS NEW

And I saw a new heaven and a new earth: for the first heaven and the first earth were passed away; and there was no more sea.
And I John saw the holy city, new Jerusalem, coming down from God out of heaven, prepared as a bride adorned for her husband.
And I heard a great voice out of heaven saying, Behold, the tabernacle of God is with men, and he will dwell with them, and they shall be his people, and God himself shall be with them, and be their God.

And God shall wipe away all tears from their eyes; and there shall be no more death, neither sorrow, nor crying, neither shall there be any more pain: for the former things are passed away.
And he that sat upon the throne said, Behold, I make all things new. And he said unto me, Write: for these words are true and faithful.

And he said unto me, It is done. I am Alpha and Omega, the beginning and the end. I will give unto him that is athirst of the fountain of the water of life freely.
He that overcometh shall inherit all things; and I will be his God, and he shall be my son.

[Revelation, Chapter 21, verses 1–7]

CHAPTER SEVEN

The Crown Jewels of English Poetry

Let the Scots sing of their Robbie Burns, the Welsh of their Dylan Thomas and the Irish of Yeats, but I will sing of the poets whose limbs were made in England, of Shakespeare, Milton, Keats, Spenser, Wordsworth, Shelley, Coleridge, Tennyson, Masefield, Browning, Marlowe, Marvel, Dryden, to name but a few; but what a treasury of literature is ours here in this tiny island! We have been described as the People of the Book and it may well be that our genius for prose and poetry has been nourished by our knowledge of the Bible.

As a child, I remember being taken by an aunt to see the Crown Jewels in the Tower of London. They were so priceless and so beautiful I was almost afraid to look. What a good thing it is that the Crown Jewels of English poetry are not under guard, encaged in iron and glass, but free for all. At any public library you can take your pick amongst the pearls, the rubies, the emeralds and the diamonds. With so many dazzling gems set out before me, where and how can I make a start? Having only a short thread on which to hang the jewels of my choice I must confine myself to a small selection.

For as far back as I can recollect William Wordsworth was my favourite poet. I loved his holy pantheism, his genius in identifying Nature with God. And I loved him because he lived out his creed in his daily life—walking in all weathers fair or foul, not necessarily for exercise but for the ecstasy of feeling at one with Nature in all her moods.

This Wordsworth worship lasted up to a few years ago when by a chain of fortuitous circumstances I found myself in the little room in which Keats died in Rome on February 23rd, 1821, at the age of 24. What I experienced in that room led me to Keats House in Hampstead, once called Wentworth Place, from which John Keats set out for Rome on September 13th, 1820, never to return. The devotion of his good friend Joseph Severn during the frightful voyage and up to the last hour of his life is a story in itself.

In the garden of Keats House, Hampstead you can see the descendant of the plum tree under which the 'Ode to a Nightingale' was written. Keats once wrote 'I think that after my death I shall be remembered amongst the great English poets', a truly prophetic thought.

Sometimes on lovely October mornings, wandering around the little streets near the Cathedral in Winchester, where it was written, I used to think that the 'Ode to Autumn' was the loveliest thing Keats ever wrote, but at other times, by the edge of the sea, watching the waves at their priest-like task of pure ablution, I have felt that Bright Star reflected to perfection the full splendour of his genius.

Inspired by his love for Fanny Brawne, finished during a brief period at Lulworth on the voyage to

Rome, the last time he ever set foot on English soil, written in his Shakespeare and given to Joseph Severn, it is a cry from a heart in love with the loveliness of Nature and sad with the desolation of his unfulfilled passion for Fanny.

Yes, Bright Star is now for me the Kohinor diamond of the Keatsian treasury.

'LINES, Composed A Few Miles Above Tintern Abbey, On Revisiting The Banks of the Wye During A Tour. July 13th, 1798.' These are the bald words used as a title for one of the finest things William Wordsworth ever wrote, but I always think of it as 'Seeing Into The Life of Things' for in this sublime piece of writing Wordsworth enriches the English language with one of its most beautiful phrases:

> While with an eye made quiet by the power
> Of harmony, and the deep power of joy,
> We see into the life of things.

This is what Wordsworth teaches us to do: to look beyond the manifestations into the meanings. To stand on the hill seeing Tintern Abbey across the Wye is to be detached from the worldliness of the world and to understand a little of what the poet meant when, reflecting upon the Ullswater daffodils he wrote of 'That inward eye which is the bliss of solitude'. To be able to see into the life of things is to look at a tree and see more than bark, trunk, boughs and leaves. Everything visible has its spiritual counterpart and it is this that Wordsworth's genius unveils to the seeing eye.

In the following brief selections from the Tintern treasure chest can be discovered pearls enough to ensure its immortality: 'The still, sad music of humanity', 'A presence that disturbs me with the joy of elevated thoughts' and 'Nature never did betray the heart that loved her'. Here are thoughts that redeem us from the commonplace and lift the mind above 'the dreary intercourse of daily life'.

> For I have learned
> To look on nature, not as in the hour
> Of thoughtless youth; but hearing oftentimes
> The still, sad music of humanity,
> Nor harsh, nor grating, though of ample power

To chasten or subdue. And I have felt
A presence that disturbs me with a joy
Of elevated thoughts; a sense sublime
Of something far more deeply interfused,
Whose dwelling is the light of setting suns,
And the round ocean and the living air,
And the blue sky, and in the mind of man;
A motion and a spirit that impels
All thinking things, all objects of all thought,
And rolls through all things.

FULL OF BLESSINGS

. . . and this prayer I make,
Knowing that Nature never did betray
The heart that loved her; 'tis her privilege,
Through all the years of this our life, to lead
From joy to joy: for she can so inform
That mind that is within us, so impress
With quietness and beauty, and so feed
With lofty thoughts, that neither evil tongues,
Rash judgments, nor the sneers of selfish men,
Nor greetings where no kindness is, nor all
The dreary intercourse of daily life,
Shall e'er prevail against us, or disturb
Our cheerful faith, that all which we behold
Is full of blessings.

INTIMATIONS OF IMMORTALITY FROM RECOLLECTIONS OF EARLY CHILDHOOD

There was a time when meadow, grove, and stream,
The earth, and every common sight,
  To me did seem
  Apparelled in celestial light,
The glory and the freshness of a dream.
It is not now as it hath been of yore,—
  Turn wheresoe'er I may,
  By night or day,
The things which I have seen I now can see no more.

The rainbow comes and goes,
And lovely is the rose;
The moon doth with delight
Look round her when the heavens are bare;
Waters on a starry night
Are beautiful and fair;
The sunshine is a glorious birth;
But yet I know, where'er I go,
That there hath passed away a glory from the earth.

[William Wordsworth, born in Cumberland, 1770; died at Rydal Mount, 1850; succeeded Southey as Poet Laureate in 1843]

A sense of communion with Nature comes and goes like the passing of the wind. Sometimes, the true Nature lover feels at one with every living thing; at others the spirit of Nature seems to be withdrawn and we walk estranged amongst familiar scenes like aliens, out of touch, not knowing the language of communication. That the sensitive soul of Wordsworth experienced the agonies of these times of withdrawal and separation is expressed sublimely in the first two stanzas of 'The Intimations of Immortality'. Writing of his boyhood in 'The Prelude' he reflects:

In many a thoughtless hour, when, from excess
Of happiness, my blood appeared to flow
For its own pleasure, and I breathed with joy.

From the same pen came the words, 'There hath passed away a glory from the earth', but I cannot believe that it was the mere passage of years that explains the change of mood. It is Life and not Time that sets the key for the alternations of delight and despair.

Our birth is but a sleep and a forgetting:
The Soul that rises with us, our life's Star,
Hath had elsewhere its setting,
And cometh from afar:

Not in entire forgetfulness,
And not in utter nakedness,
But trailing clouds of glory do we come
From God, who is our home:
Heaven lies about us in our infancy!
Shades of the prison-house begin to close
Upon the growing Boy,
But He beholds the light, and whence it flows,
He sees it in his joy;
The Youth, who daily farther from the east
Must travel, still is Nature's Priest,
And by the vision splendid
Is on his way attended;
At length the Man perceives it die away,
And fade into the light of common day.

[5th Stanza from 'The Intimations of Immortality']

TO A SKYLARK

Ethereal minstrel! pilgrim of the sky!
Dost thou despise the earth where cares abound?
Or, while the wings aspire, are heart and eye
Both with thy nest upon the dewy ground?
The nest which thou canst drop into at will,
Those quivering wings composed, that music still!
Leave to the nightingale her shady wood;
A privacy of glorious light is thine;
Whence thou dost pour upon the world a flood
Of harmony, with instinct more divine;
Type of the wise who soar, but never roam;
True to the kindred points of Heaven and Home!

[From 'Poems of the Imagination',
by William Wordsworth]

COMPOSED UPON WESTMINSTER BRIDGE, SEPTEMBER 3rd, 1802

Earth has not anything to show more fair:
Dull would he be of soul who could pass by

A sight so touching in its majesty:
This City now doth, like a garment, wear
The beauty of the morning; silent, bare,
Ships, towers, domes, theatres, and temples lie
Open unto the fields, and to the sky;
All bright and glittering in the smokeless air.
Never did sun more beautifully steep
In his first splendour, valley, rock, or hill;
Ne'er saw I, never felt a calm so deep!
The river glideth at his own sweet will:
Dear God! the very houses seem asleep;
And all that mighty heart is lying still!

[William Wordsworth]

ODE TO A NIGHTINGALE

My heart aches, and a drowsy numbness pains
My sense, as though of hemlock I had drunk,
Or emptied some dull opiate to the drains
One minute past, and Lethe-wards had sunk:
'Tis not through envy of thy happy lot,
But being too happy in thy happiness,—
That thou, light-wingèd Dryad of the trees,
  In some melodious plot
Of beechen green, and shadows numberless,
Singest of summer in full-throated ease.

O, for a draught of vintage! that hath been
Cool'd a long age in the deep-delved earth,
Tasting of Flora and the country green,
Dance, and Provençal song, and sunburnt mirth!
O for a beaker full of the warm South,
Full of the true, the blushful Hippocrene,
With beaded bubbles winking at the brim,
  And purple-stained mouth;
That I might drink, and leave the world unseen,
And with thee fade away into the forest dim:

Fade far away, dissolve, and quite forget
What thou among the leaves has never known,
The weariness, the fever, and the fret
Here, where men sit and hear each other groan;
Where palsy shakes a few, sad, last grey hairs,
Where youth grows pale, and spectre-thin, and dies;
Where but to think is to be full of sorrow
  And leaden-eyed despairs,
Where beauty cannot keep her lustrous eyes,
Or new Love pine at them beyond to-morrow.

Away! away! for I will fly to thee,
Not charioted by Bacchus and his pards,
But on the viewless wings of Poesy,
Though the dull brain perplexes and retards:
Already with thee! tender is the night,
And haply the Queen-Moon is on her throne,
Cluster'd around by all her starry Fays;
  But here there is no light,
Save what from heaven is with the breezes blown
Through verdurous glooms and winding mossy ways.

I cannot see what flowers are at my feet,
Nor what soft incense hangs upon the boughs,
But, in embalmbéd darkness, guess each sweet
Wherewith the seasonable month endows
The grass, the thicket, and the fruit-tree wild;
White hawthorn and the pastoral eglantine;
Fast fading violets cover'd up in leaves;
  And mid-May's eldest child
The coming musk-rose, full of dewy wine,
The murmurous haunt of flies on summer eves.

Darkling I listen; and, for many a time
I have been half in love with easeful Death,
Call'd him soft names in many a mused rhyme,
To take into the air my quiet breath;
Now more than ever seems it rich to die,
To cease upon the midnight with no pain,
While thou art pouring forth thy soul abroad

In such an ecstasy!
Still wouldst thou sing, and I have ears in vain—
To thy high requiem become a sod.

Thou wast not born for death, immortal Bird!
No hungry generations tread thee down;
The voice I hear this passing night was heard
In ancient days by emperor and clown:
Perhaps the self-same song that found a path
Through the sad heart of Ruth, when, sick for home,
She stood in tears amid the alien corn;
The same that oft-times hath
Charm'd magic casements, opening on the foam
Of perilous seas, in faery lands forlorn.

Forlorn! the very word is like a bell
To toll me back from thee to my sole self!
Adieu! the fancy cannot cheat so well
As she is fam'd to do, deceiving elf.
Adieu! adieu! thy plaintive anthem fades
Past the near meadows, over the still stream
Up the hill-side; and now 'tis buried deep
In the next valley-glades:
Was it a vision, or a waking dream?
Fled is that music:—Do I wake or sleep?

[John Keats (1795–1821) (written in the garden of Wentworth Place, Hampstead)]

ODE ON A GRECIAN URN

Thou still unravish's bride of quietness,
Thou foster-child of silence and slow time,
Sylvan historian, who canst thus express
A flowery tale more sweetly than our rhyme:
What leaf-fring'd legend haunts about thy shape
Of deities or mortals, or of both,
In Tempe or the dales of Arcady?
What men or gods are these? What maidens loth?
What mad pursuit? What struggle to escape?
What pipes and timbrels? What wild ecstasy?

Heard melodies are sweet, but those unheard
  Are sweeter; therefore, ye soft pipes, play on;
Not to the sensual ear, but, more endear'd,
  Pipe to the spirit ditties of no tone:
Fair youth, beneath the trees, thou canst not leave
  Thy song, nor ever can those trees be bare;
  Bold Lover, never, never canst thou kiss,
Though winning near the goal—yet, do not grieve;
  She cannot fade, though thou hast not thy bliss,
  For ever wilt thou love and she be fair!

Ah, happy, happy boughs! that cannot shed
  Your leaves, nor ever bid the Spring adieu;
And, happy melodist, unwearied,
  For ever piping songs for ever new;
More happy love! more happy, happy love!
  For ever warm and still to be enjoy'd,
    For ever panting, and for ever young;
All breathing human passion far above,
  That leaves a heart high-sorrowful and cloy'd,
  A burning forehead, and a parching tongue.

Who are these coming to the sacrifice?
  To what green altar, O mysterious priest,
Leads't thou that heifer lowing at the skies,
  And all her silken flanks with garlands drest?
What little town by river or sea shore,
  Or mountain-built with peaceful citadel
  Is emptied of its folk, this pious morn?
And, little town, thy streets for evermore
  Will silent be; and not a soul to tell
    Why thou are desolate, can e'er return.

O Attic shape! Fair attitude! with brede
  Of marble men and maidens overwrought,
With forest branches and the trodden weed;
  Thou, silent form, dost tease us out of thought
As doth eternity: Cold Pastoral!
  When old age shall this generation waste,

Thou shalt remain in midst of other woe
Than ours, a friend to man, to whom thou say'st
'Beauty is truth, truth beauty,'—that is all
Ye know on earth, and all ye need to know.

[John Keats (written at Hampstead)]

ODE TO AUTUMN

Season of mists and mellow fruitfulness,
Close bosom-friend of the maturing sun;
Conspiring with him how to load and bless
With fruit the vines that round the thatch-eaves run;
To bend with apples the moss'd cottage-trees
And fill all fruit with ripeness to the core;
To swell the gourd and plump the hazel shells
With a sweet kernel; to set budding more,
And still more, later flowers for the bees,
Until they think warm days will never cease,
For summer has o'er-brimmed their clammy cells.

[John Keats—(written at Winchester)]

Lack of space forbids me to go beyond these few lines. It is a mere snippet cut from the tapestry of Keats's ode with its rich autumnal tones. The 'Eve of St Agnes' must also be passed over, but not without lingering for a few seconds on those incomparable lines:

Numb were the Beadsman's fingers while he told
His rosary and while his frosted breath,
Like pious incense from a censer old
Seem'd taking flight for heaven without a death
Past the sweet Virgin's picture, while his prayer he saith.

And what a delight it would have been to have included in full 'La Belle Dame Sans Merci' with its haunting beauty and its fairylike, unearthly enchantment captured in such lines as:

And there I shut her wild wild eyes
With kisses four.

Keats's last sonnet, 'Bright Star', written for Fanny Brawne whom he loved and from whom he knew he was parting for ever when he left Wentworth Place, Hampstead, is a jewel of poetic perfection. It was completed during the first part of that fateful voyage to Naples in the *Maria Crowther* and written by Keats in Joseph Severn's Shakespeare. What a treasure!

BRIGHT STAR

Bright star! would I were steadfast as thou art—
Not in lone splendour hung aloft the night
And watching, with eternal lids apart,
Like Nature's patient, sleepless Eremite,
The moving waters at their priestlike task
Of pure ablution round earth's human shores,
Or gazing on the new soft fallen mask
Of snow upon the mountains and the moors—
No—yet still steadfast, still unchangeable,
Pillow'd upon my fair love's ripening breast,
To feel forever its soft fall and swell,
Awake forever in a sweet unrest,
Still, still to hear her tender-taken breath,
And so live ever—or else swoon to death.

The fifty-five stanzas of 'Adonais', Shelley's elegy on the death of Keats, is like a symphony, a series of movements threaded with unforgettable passages that inflame the imagination and haunt the memory. The whole of it cannot be heard and assimilated at a single reading. Sudden phrases grip the mind, checking the flow of emotion, giving pause for sweetnesses and sadnesses to get at the heart. Words such as the following stop thought in its tracks. To leap from line to line without a break is to miss some of the music of its mingled themes.

Peace, peace! he is not dead, he doth not sleep—
He hath awakened from the dream of life—

Stanza 39

He has outsoared the shadow of our night;
Envy and calumny, and hate and pain,
And that unrest which men miscall delight,
Can touch him not and torture not again;
From the contagion of the world's slow stain
He is secure. . . .

Stanza 40

He is a portion of the loveliness
Which once he made more lovely:

Stanza 43

These are but fleeting flashes from the glory of Adonais. For me the greatest line of all comes in the 49th stanza with its reference to 'a light of laughing flowers'. The delicate almost fairylike touch of this thought breaks in upon the sombre theme of the grave like a sudden flicker of sunshine in a dark room.

Go thou to Rome,—at once the paradise,
The grave, the city, and the wilderness;
And where its wrecks like shattered mountains rise,
And flowering weeds and fragrant copses dress
The bones of Desolation's nakedness,
Pass, till the Spirit of the spot shall lead
Thy footsteps to a slope of green access,
Where, like an infant's smile, over the dead
A light of laughing flowers along the grass is spread.

In one of the quiet interludes of fever as Keats lay still and at peace he said to Joseph Severn, 'I feel the flowers growing over me'. Shelley with true vision caught a glint of those 'laughing flowers', for even in the winter violets grew there in thick profusion. The following year the ashes of Shelley's own heart were to be buried in this little Protestant cemetery, and fifty-eight years later the body of the faithful Severn was laid beside his beloved friend John Keats. How sacred to an Englishman is this quiet little garden of the dead where the 'keen pyramid' of Cestius cuts its incongruous wedge into the blue of the Roman sky!

Give me my scallop-shell of quiet,
  My staff of faith to walk upon,
My scrip of joy, immortal diet,
  My bottle of salvation,
My gown of glory, hope's true gage;
  And thus I'll take my pilgrimage.

[Sir Walter Raleigh (born in Devon 1552; beheaded in 1618)]

How strange that a man whose life had been bold, exciting and adventurous and which had come to a violent and cruel end should have written what I have always felt to be one of the loveliest poems in the English language. It is good to reflect that in the turmoil of his times he should have discovered 'the scallop-shell of quiet'.

And did those feet in ancient time
Walk upon England's mountains green?
And was the holy Lamb of God
On England's pleasant pastures seen?

And did the Countenance divine
Shine forth upon our clouded hills?
And was Jerusalem builded here
Among these dark Satanic mills?

Bring me my bow of burning gold!
Bring me my arrows of desire!
Bring me my spear! O clouds, unfold!
Bring me my Chariot of fire!

I will not cease from mental fight,
Nor shall my sword sleep in my hand,
Till we have built Jerusalem
In England's green and pleasant land.

[William Blake (1757–1827)]

The belief that our Lord came to Britain at some time during the eighteen hidden years between the age of twelve and thirty lingers in the West Country with a persistence that goes deeper than the desire to cherish an old legend. Joseph of Arimathea, to whom he was related on Mary's side and in whose tomb he was buried, was a wealthy merchant who came frequently to transact business with the famous tin miners of Cornwall. As Jesus was fatherless, it is not beyond the bounds of possibility that Joseph would have brought his young kinsman with him on one of these voyages. Evidence that our Lord visited the Isle of Avalon where the Druidic religion had already prepared the ground for the coming of the Messiah, is supported by a letter written by St Augustine to Pope Gregory in 597 in which he writes: 'In the western confines of Britain there is a certain royal island (Glastonbury) of large extent, surrounded by water, abounding in all the beauties of nature and necessaries of life. In it the first neophytes of Catholic Law (converts or ministers) found a church constructed by no human art, but divinely constructed, for the salvation of His people. The Almighty has made it manifest by many miracles and mysterious visitations that He continues to watch over it as sacred to Himself, and to Mary, the Mother of God.' Could this have been the little wattle and daub church found there by Joseph of Arimathea on his arrival in Avalon, the Isle of Apples, the sacred fruit of the Druids, three years after the crucifixion, and over which he erected between A.D. 38–39 the first Christian church above ground in the world, built on the lines of the Tabernacle sixty feet long and twenty-six feet wide? It is interesting to note that at the Council of Pisa in 1417, the Council of Constance in 1419 and the Council of Siena in 1423 it was stated that the British Church took precedence of all other Churches, being founded by Joseph of Arimathea, immediately after the Passion of Christ. And in the *Morning Post* of March 27th, 1931, it was recorded that Pope Pius XI, addressing the Mayors of Bath, Colchester and Dorchester, along with a hundred and fifty members of the Friends of Italy Society, said that St Paul, not Pope Gregory, first introduced Christianity to Britain. That must have fallen strangely upon some ears, but the truth was even stranger.

Perhaps Blake was not indulging in a flight of poetic fantasy when he asked his question 'Was the holy Lamb of God on England's pleasant pastures seen?' Can it be mere chance that Blake's poem set to music has become a second national anthem? Did those feet in ancient time truly walk the green hills of Somerset?

THE MINISTRY OF ANGELS

And is there care in Heaven? And is there love
In heavenly spirits to these creatures base,
That may compassion of their evils move?
There is: else much more wretched were the case
Of men than beasts: but oh the exceeding grace
Of highest God, that loves his creatures so,
And all his works with mercy doth embrace,
That blessed angels he sends to and fro,
To serve to wicked man, to serve his foe!

How oft do they their silver bowers leave
To come to succour us that succour want!
How oft do they with golden pinions cleave
The flittering skies, like flying pursuivant,
Against foul fiends, to aid us militant!

They for us fight, they watch and duly ward,
And their bright squadrons round about us plant;
And all for love and nothing for reward:
O, why should heavenly God to men have such regard?

[Edmund Spenser (1553–99)]

To every man his guardian angel. At the beginning of every new day it is wise to pray that he be quick in his duty of averting bodily harm and mental dangers in these times when death in one form or another lurks at every corner.

To lift the latch on the old green garden gate at Farringford on the Isle of Wight and follow the track along which Tennyson used to take his afternoon walk is to open a gate into a fairyland; it is as if the wild flowers clustering about the paths wear little haloes knowing whose feet once trod about their roots.

THE SNOWDROP

Many, many welcomes
February fair-maid,
Ever as of old time,
Solitary firstling,
Coming in the cold time,
Prophet of the gay time,
Prophet of the May time,
Prophet of the roses,
Many, many welcomes
February fair-maid!

From 'Maud' such lines as:

There has fallen a splendid tear
From the passion-flower at the gate

and from 'The Princess',

The moan of doves in immemorial elms
And murmuring of innumerable bees.

breathe the spirit of a man in tune with all things lovely. I have fed on the romance of the 'Idylls of the King' for as long as I can remember and thrilled to the sound of

Wearing the white flower of a blameless life
Before a thousand peering littlenesses,
In that fierce light that beats about a throne,
And blackens every blot;
[from the Dedication in 'Idylls of the King'.]

The 'Charge of the Light Brigade' evokes a personal memory of my grandfather who used to stand with his back to the fire and recite it after tea every year on Christmas Day. It was as ritualistic as the pulling of the crackers and the finding of the threepenny piece in the pudding, but the poem that has always meant most to me has been 'Crossing the Bar', the last in my beautiful Globe edition and probably the best known and best loved of anything Tennyson ever wrote. It is a gentle reminder of the reality of the fact of death which confronts everyone, young or old, no matter how many mental barriers he or she may erect against its intrusion. It should be read to the dying in homes and hospitals where many a lonely soul has to part company with its familiar body with no friends or relatives present to ease the pangs of severance. The calm faith that pervades this poem is a more potent tranquilliser than the customary dope so often now given by doctors to the dying, depriving them of the great experience of dissolution. The peace conveyed in the poem is not the calmness of a negative resignation; it is born rather of a positive affirmation, not in the mere continuance of existence, but in the hope of seeing the face of One who said, 'I am the resurrection'.

There are recollections that cling about the mind which no time can expunge. One such is conjured up for me whenever 'Crossing the Bar' is heard or read. I am transported on the wings of imagination back to an evening shortly after the Second World War when I was leaning on the deck rail of a small ship on the Zuider Zee listening to the faraway sound of a church bell coming across a great still sheet of water which seemed to have no horizon. Everything in Tennyson's poem was gathered up into that exquisite moment: the sunset, the motionless water and the distant bell. And when I hear the one clear call for my own embarkation I pray that my mind will still be open to the inflowing of that beautiful and unforgettable memory.

CROSSING THE BAR

Sunset and evening star,
  And one clear call for me!
And may there be no moaning of the bar,
  When I put out to sea.

But such a tide as moving seems asleep
  Too full for sound and foam,
When that which drew from out the boundless deep
  Turns again home.

Twilight and evening bell,
  And after that the dark!
And may there be no sadness of farewell,
  When I embark.

For tho' from out our bourne of Time and Place
  The flood may bear me far,
I hope to see my Pilot face to face
  When I have crost the bar.

[Lord Alfred Tennyson, Poet Laureate (1809–92)]

I have been so carried away by my love for the poets of the past that there is little space left for including more than one of my latter-day favourites. It seems to me that modern poetry lacks spiritual impetus, but, like water-lilies with their roots in the mud, many lovely poems have come floating to the surface from such writers as Alice Meynell, Walter De La Mare, Victoria Sackville-West, Rupert Brooke, W. H. Davies and G. K. Chesterton, to name only a few.

The cross on the back of a donkey never fails to remind me of G. K. Chesterton's sublime poem with its reference to 'The tattered outlaw of the earth', but Harold Monro's 'Overheard On A Saltmarsh' is, in my opinion, the most beautiful poem that has come out of this materialistic and unromantic century. It must be read aloud if the full meaning with all its emotional overtones and undertones is to be conveyed. The language is frugal, imperative and passionate. All the unfulfilled longings of the human heart, the agonies of denial and the bitterness of unsatisfied passion seem to have been gathered up into a single despairing cry for a handful of green glass beads.

OVERHEARD ON A SALTMARSH

Nymph, nymph, what are your beads?
  Green glass, goblin. Why do you stare at them?
Give them me.
          No.
Give them me. Give them me.
          No.
Then I will howl all night in the reeds,
Lie in the mud and howl for them.
Goblin, why do you love them so?

They are better than stars or water,
Better than voices of winds that sing,
Better than any man's fair daughter,
Your green glass beads on a silver ring.
Hush, I stole them out of the moon.
Give me your beads. I desire them.
I will howl in a deep lagoon
For your green glass beads, I love them so.
Give them me. Give them.
                    No.

[Harold Monro (1879–1932)]